The
Best
of
Elton
Trueblood

The
Best
of
Elton
Trueblood

An Anthology

Edited and with an Introduction
by JAMES R. NEWBY

**impact
books**

Nashville, Tennessee

PUBLISHER'S NOTE

Truth knows no boundaries of time or space. Through the ages, thinking men—Socrates, Aristotle, St. Augustine—have sought truth, tried it, dissected it, distilled it, and bequeathed it to succeeding generations of man.

In this tradition, we have preserved in one volume the quintessence of one of the foremost Christian thinkers of this century. Dr. Elton Trueblood is philosopher, poet, and dean of American religious writers. Like the ancients, his diligence and discipline have carved for him a place in history.

Now, at the pinnacle of his writing career and in the twilight years of his life, it is fitting that Dr. Trueblood should pass the torch to the runners of the future. One who has accepted that challenge is James R. Newby, Dr. Trueblood's associate, who has compiled under ten Trueblood Topics, his practical philosophy which is still relevant and cogent to today's readers.

It is with pride that we present this distinctive work which, like its author, is destined for greatness.

JOHN T. BENSON, III

CONTENTS

INTRODUCTION

Elton Trueblood has lived every day of the twentieth century. He was born on December 12, 1900, in a farming community of southern Iowa, and was reared in a strict Quaker home where "going to Meeting" was as much a part of life as eating or sleeping. The disciplined atmosphere of his growing years provided a strong foundation for his career as a college professor and Christian author, since the living of a disciplined life has been the basis for his pursuit of excellence in both teaching and writing. In his beautifully written autobiography, *While It Is Day*, he describes how the Christian Endeavor Society of the local Friends Church helped him to undertake his first voluntary discipline:

> I signed the pledge to take some part, other than singing, in every meeting of the Society, and also to engage daily in both Bible reading and prayer. Honoring my signature, I kept the promise, thus early learning something of the power released by the voluntary acceptance of discipline . . .[1]

Besides learning the value of discipline, Elton Trueblood's Quaker upbringing implanted within him an understanding of Christianity that has affected the whole of his adult life, and has influenced every major piece of his writing. He was taught at an early age that the essence of Quakerism is merely the attempt to exemplify the basic Christian faith. He believes, as did William Penn, that Quakerism is simply "Christianity writ plain," and a careful study of Dr. Trueblood's writings will show that his career

has been devoted to helping people go beyond the ceremonies and symbols of any ritualistic faith, to this basic
understanding of essential Christianity. He is convinced
that, by carefully studying the faith of the New Testament,
the contemporary church will, in turn, be revived, since
Christians can thus judge their mild religion by the
dynamic faith of the Early Church. To be as much like
Christ as we can is the Christian's goal, and if this goal is to
be realized, the believer must understand the basics of his
faith. The writings of Elton Trueblood help to point the
seeker to the vitality of the Christian message, thus encouraging him to become a finder.

Having been in the public eye for half a century, at this
stage in his career Elton Trueblood is finding the beautiful
surroundings of Earlham College most enjoyable and
profitable. His home, Virginia Cottage, is located on the
northeast corner of the campus, and his study, Teague
Library, is situated in a separate building across the walk, in
clear view from the side window of his living room. Immediately behind his home and study is the International
Headquarters of Yokefellows, an interdenominational organization of committed Christians, founded by Dr. Trueblood in 1949. This is where the man of letters now spends
most of his time, and where he continues to influence the
world of Christian thought and action, welcoming students
and visitors who have been touched by his writings.

One of the curious observations to be made in these, the
autumn years of Dr. Trueblood's life, is the observation that
his popularity as a speaker and writer has not diminished
with the years, but has, in actuality, steadily increased.
Many people are discovering that the danger Elton Trueblood foretold over thirty-five years ago, is now a frightening reality. The "cut-flower" civilization, which was so
eloquently described in his book, *The Predicament Of Modern
Man*, in 1944, is now coming to pass. The words which we
find most prophetic, and which strike at the heart of our
current crisis, are as follows:

> The terrible danger of our time consists in the fact that ours is a cut-flower civilization. Beautiful as cut flowers may be, and much as we may use our ingenuity to keep them looking fresh for a while, they will eventually die, and they die because they are severed from their sustaining roots. We are trying to maintain the dignity of the individual apart from the deep faith that every man is made in God's image and is therefore precious in God's eyes . . .[2]

With these words Dr. Trueblood guides his readers to the heart of our human predicament. We are a society trying to live in the dungeon of subjectivity, cut off from the living God, and, as a result, the current generation often denies even the existence of any objective moral order. "What we need," he continues, "is not an assertion of our own ideals, but contact with the eternally real . . . What men need, if they are to overcome their lethargy and weakness, is some contact with the real world in which moral values are centered in the nature of things. This is the love of God, for which men have long shown themselves willing to live or to die. The only sure way in which we can transcend our human relativities is by obedience to the absolute and eternal God."[3]

Without fear of ridicule from the liberal educational establishment, Elton Trueblood boldly proclaims himself an "Evangelical Christian." He considers a "non-evangelical Christian" a contradiction in terms. He came to this understanding of the faith after a great deal of study, and particularly following his reading of C.S. Lewis. In his early ministry Dr. Trueblood often mentioned Christ in his messages and writings, but he did not emphasize His uniqueness. It was C.S. Lewis who finally "shocked" him out of his unexamined liberalism. "In reading Lewis," he writes, "I could not escape the conclusion that the popular view of Christ as being a teacher, and *only* a teacher, has within it a self-contradiction that cannot be resolved. I saw, in short, that conventional liberalism cannot survive rigorous and rational analysis. What Lewis and a few others made me face was the hard fact that if Christ was only a teacher, then he was a false one, since, in His teaching, He claimed to be *more*."[4]

There are a number of outstanding aspects of the Trueblood personality that should be examined in this introduction, and will prove to be helpful to the reader as he begins his pilgrimage through this anthology. We must begin by asking the question of why Elton Trueblood stands as a giant in the field of religious writing and thinking. What is the secret of his highly successful career as an author, teacher, and minister-at-large? This question is not easily answered, but we can begin to understand the greatness of the Trueblood personality when we look at a combination of factors working in conjunction with one another, rather as isolated elements.

The first recognizable quality of genuine magnitude is *discipline*, a quality, as mentioned before, that was developed at a very young age. Elton Trueblood is the most disciplined man I have ever known. He has discovered the rewards of self-discipline, since he knows full well that inherent in the human race is the tendency toward laziness, which, if left unchecked, becomes sinful waste. He regards time as a sacred gift, and uses every minute of every day as a witness to the glory of God. He is a very structured individual who maintains a schedule that would weaken men half his age. Since he discovered early in his life that he is most productive in the morning, he retires at 10:00 P.M. each night, and is in his study by 7:00 A.M. every morning. His most valuable time for writing is between 7:00 A.M. and noon. This command over his life is the main reason he has been able to produce so much. It may surprise some of his readers to learn that all of Trueblood's prolific writing is produced longhand, with a fountain pen.

Coupled with this strict discipline is his *availability to students*. His very structured life and his openness to the possibility of change, if he is needed somewhere else, might at first seem to be contradictory. But, upon further evaluation, one can see that they are complementary. Dr. Trueblood's discipline enables him to have time for those who need his help! Hard at work on a manuscript or a speech, I have seen him put all of that work aside and devote his undivided attention to a student who is having difficulty in his studies. His library is always open, and, regardless of whether he is preparing a sermon or grading a philosophy student's paper, he always finds time to help anyone who comes to his door.

Another very important aspect of the Trueblood profile is his *devotion to academic excellence.* He is unswerving in his dedication to the development of the mind. His own career as an academician has taken him through the halls of Harvard and Johns Hopkins, the most rigorous philosophical schools in the country. Under the tutelage of the famous Arthur O. Lovejoy of Johns Hopkins, and Willard L. Sperry of Harvard, Elton Trueblood has acquired a deep appreciation for hard, disciplined study. Since we have learned that nothing of value is gained without hard work, those of us who are his students are especially aware of this important aspect of emphasis. This concern is given expression in his essay on "The Redemption Of The College," where he pleads for a new reformation on the campuses of Christian schools:

> Part of our purpose is the production of Christian intellectuals, men and women who can combine the love of God with the love of learning. If this is not done in the way of excellence, it will not be done at all. The option provided by the existence of the Christian college should be harder rather than easier, when compared with its alternatives, for we are in a more ambitious enterprise than are our competitors. This, however, is something which we have sometimes failed to realize, but unless we recognize it, we shall not survive and furthermore, we shall not deserve to survive.[5]

Always he is pushing Christians toward the standards of excellence, striving to equip them for the hard task of defending their faith in the midst of the arrogant paganism that infects our age. He is a Christian encourager, and has taken for his golden text the words of St. Paul found in I Thessalonians 5:11, "Therefore encourage one another, and build one another up" (RSV). One of the best examples of Dr. Trueblood's fulfilling this command of Paul is found in the way he encourages students of all ages to excel.

Coupled with this demand for scholarly achievement is Elton Trueblood's *sensitivity and openness in the worship of God*. Intellectualism, he has shown, does not necessarily mean dull formalism, since he believes and has demonstrated, that clear, hard thinking can be combined with a warm, worshipful heart. Thus, he feels equally comfortable in the midst of a philosophical or theological debate, or singing, "Jesus, Lover Of My Soul" in a village service of worship. The intellectual dimension of the Christian faith, he insists, does not have to be separated from a meaningful Christ-centered experience of reverence. Thinking and feeling in the religious life is a combination that Elton Trueblood has consciously sought to keep in balance.

One more combination in the Trueblood personality must be noted. Although he is a serious, philosophical thinker and teacher, he has a penetrating *sense of humor*. While he realizes the tragedy of so much of our human predicament, and has sought through the medium of logical thinking to help people better to understand this often difficult and complicated life, he has never lost his perspective and is always ready to hear or share a funny story. Humor, he feels, provides meaningful interludes in the continuous process of rigorous thinking. He has often used the quotation from Abraham Lincoln, who when asked one day why he was always laughing, responded in characteristic Lincoln style, "If I did not laugh, I would cry." Elton Trueblood has made Abraham Lincoln one of his most influential models, and has written an important book concerning the Great Emancipator, entitled, *Abraham Lincoln: Theologian Of American Anguish*. Nowhere does the similarity of these two men become more apparent than in the way they have faced both the triumphs and tragedies of life, combining a sense of serious concern with a humorous disposition.

In the style of Samuel Johnson, another of Dr. Trueblood's models, he is a devout moralist. Although his writing is prophetic, always warning his readers about their condition and the condition of the world, it also inspires reassurance and trust. Hence, for the past forty-five years, these who have been reading Elton Trueblood have not only been led to adjust their thinking in a logical way, but they have also experienced a sense of relief in the hope of redemption. I believe this to be the greatest single reason why Elton Trueblood's writing has remained so popular for so many years, and is the way in which his conjunct life is best expressed. He is honest with his public concerning the dire predicament of our time, but, along with this note of prophetic insight, the reader is always lifted by a resounding sense of hope.

In this literary style Elton Trueblood has no rival. His ability to capture the human situation, and then to call on Christians to move from complacency to commitment in making a response, while, at the same time, helping us to develop a sustaining trust and hope in Jesus Christ, is the work of a special kind of genius. Where most religious authors are tempted to isolate the pessimistic side of human existence, with little or no regard given to the bright spots, or to create a false trust in an empty optimism that does not mention the darker aspects of life, Elton Trueblood combines an emphasis upon both. Because he appreciates the necessity of paradox, his writing is both disturbing and refreshing at the same time. He cuts through the bleakness of contemporary decay to the essentials of Christian hope, while keeping steadily in mind the problems of decay. This combination of optimism and pessimism, realism and idealism, makes Elton Trueblood unique in his field.

Elton Trueblood, the dean of American religious writers, has been one of the most prolific authors of the twentieth century. Thirty-one volumes, countless articles, and numerous lectures have been the products of his pen. This man who is deeply concerned about human life has chosen the discipline of writing to record these concerns and insights into the human situation. His writing has not been primarily for the person who wishes to remain aloof from the world's problems, secure in the ivory tower of theological confusion. He writes, instead, for the committed Christian seeker who needs a plan to follow, and an encouraging word for a depressed spirit. The concerns about which Elton Trueblood writes have been nourished in the belief that Christians are called to be participants and not mere spectators, to be actively working from a Christian perspective toward solutions to the problems of our world, and not just bench warmers on the sidelines. He does not offer his readers words that will only comfort them; he gives them a challenge from which they cannot easily turn away.

"We must work the works of him who sent me, while it is day; night comes when no one can work" (John 9:4, RSV). These familiar words from the Gospel of John have been used by Elton Trueblood in selecting a title for his autobiography. At seventy-nine years of age, Dr. Trueblood knows that the night of his earthly life is drawing ever closer. Secure in this knowledge, he has taken a lesson from Samuel Johnson, who stressed the importance of living each day to its fullest, one at a time. A slowed, but still active, schedule of speaking engagements around the country continues to be an important ministry, as is the joy of conversing with visitors from far and near who drop in to see him in his beautiful library. But there is now a note of finality in his speech, a sensing that his earthly years are coming to an end. "A philosopher," he says, quoting Socrates, "is always engaged in the process of dying."

It seems appropriate at this point in the life of Elton Trueblood, and at this time in the history of the Christian faith, that an anthology reflecting the best of Trueblood's works be published. The public is eager for a sign of hope in this world of despair, a challenge instead of pablum. The words of Dr. Trueblood are sure to offer them this message of bold encouragement.

Here, compiled in a logical sequence of "Trueblood Topics," the reader will find the best, written by a master of words for the glory of God. I believe that those already acquainted with the writings of Elton Trueblood will find in these pages a valuable collection, and those who are now being introduced to a great Christian thinker will not be disappointed.

Richmond, Indiana   JAMES R. NEWBY
Labor Day, 1979

---

[1]Elton Trueblood, *While It Is Day,* (New York: Harper and Row, 1974), p. 15.
[2]Elton Trueblood, *The Predicament Of Modern Man,* (New York: Harper and Row, 1944), p. 59.
[3]Ibid. pp. 60-61.
[3]Ibid. pp. 60-61.
[4]*While It Is Day,* p. 99.
[5]Elizabeth Newby, *A Philosopher's Way: Essays And Addresses Of Elton Trueblood,* (Nashville: Broadman Press, 1978), p. 123.

Chapter One

THE CENTRALITY
OF COMMITMENT

*N*owhere is the clarity of Elton Trueblood's thinking and sense of conviction more apparent than in his understanding of Christian commitment. He believes that mild religion is the greatest threat to contemporary Christianity, and is a far cry from the dynamic model of the Early Church. In the words which follow, the reader will be challenged to reassess the centrality of his commitment to Jesus Christ and, in the process, he will be taught a better understanding of what it means to be a Christian.

J.R.N.

Committed Christians are a minority at the present time! This is true, not merely in the world at large, but in the Western world as well, and specifically in the United States of America. Though there is a widespread failure to understand this significant fact, the evidence for it is abundant. A great part of the weakness of the Christian movement stems from the miscalculation both of its strength and of the degree of its acceptance.

When we recognize how numerous the alternatives are, we are not really surprised that Christianity is a minority movement, even in the heart of the West. In addition to the systems already mentioned there is the cult of the New Left, and racism, and the various forms of militant nationalism. But the greatest single alternative is that of a conventionalized association with the Christian heritage which is best described as mild religion. There is no doubt that this accounts for the largest part of the nominal memberships in the local churches. This mild Christianity is largely separated from the Bible, which seems to many to be more of a burden than a help.

Nearly all of the representatives of mild Christianity think of themselves as antiPuritan, though the number of those who really know what the dynamic Puritan faith was in the seventeenth century seems to be few. To caricature the Puritan ethic and to reject it without genuine examination is particularly inept, especially when we think of the central fire represented by John Milton, whose creative freedom arose, not in spite of, but as a consequence of his disciplined faith.

The committed Christian is not now thrown to the lions, as were the Christians in Rome long ago, but there are, nevertheless, subtle forms of contemporary persecution. A man who takes Christ seriously is often looked upon as a hopeless fossil and is considered an enthusiast or a fanatic. In short, he is an oddity.

By commitment is meant the acceptance of convictions, not merely by intellectual assent, but by a full act of the will. The fundamental insight of Blaise Pascal, that faith is not supine acceptance of dogma, but rather something in the nature of a gamble, has been accepted by almost all subsequent thinkers. Religion, as many of us understand it, is not the acceptance of conventional standards of behavior and it is not primarily an effort to save our own puny souls; it is the exciting venture of faith in which we bet that God really is, that this is His world. and that He is like Jesus Christ.

It is the essence of a gamble that the gambler either wins or loses; he is either right or wrong. There is no middle ground. So it is with our supreme gamble. Our faith is either true to reality or it is a horrible delusion. If it is not true, it is an evil.

Commitment means willingness to take the plunge, to run the risk of seeming ridiculous if we turn out to be wrong. It is, of course, not a *wild* leap, since there is so much of a wholly intellectual nature to support our position, but, in the end, it is always a leap. We cannot remain forever on the springboard poised for the leap. To refuse to decide is itself one decision and essentially a negative decision.

Here, then, is the first plank in our platform. We seek groups of genuinely committed men and women, men and women who continue to be perplexed and doubtful in many areas of their experience but who are willing to follow one major clue wherever it may lead. Such people will believe that God has a purpose for the world, so that there is potential meaning in history. Their greatest desire is to learn that purpose and to carry it forward. People who understand their religion as absolute commitment to what is recognized as absolutely worthy cannot fail to recognize their need of help in knowing what is absolutely worthy.

There have been such various objects of supreme loyalty; how are we to choose between them? Increasingly, through the centuries, we have found in the life, teachings and death of Jesus Christ a convincing answer. He, of all, inspires our full confidence. A Christian is one who will stake everything on this confidence. We do not know all the answers, and we are very sure that there is more truth still waiting to break forth, but we are willing to risk our present and eternal destiny on the conviction that the light seen in the face of Jesus Christ is the surest light we can know.

When we think that religion is what goes on in a building of recognizable ecclesiastical architecture, the damage comes in the perfectly natural human tendency to minimize religion in *other* places. When we think of religion as what transpires on Sunday morning, the harm lies in the tendency to suppose that what goes on at other times, in factories and offices, is not equally religious. When we think of religion as the professional responsibility of priest, clergymen, and rabbis, the major harm lies in the consequent minimizing of the religious responsibility of *other* men and women. The harm of too much localizing of religious responsibility in a few—however dedicated they may be—is that it gives the rank and file a freedom from responsibility which they ought not to be able to enjoy.

The major danger of our contemporary religion, then, is that it makes small what ought to be large. By segregating religion in place or time or personnel, we make religion relatively trivial, concerned with only a part of experience when it ought to be concerned with the *whole* of life. Whenever the Church means merely a building on the corner, or a special kind of service, or a man with a round collar, the salt has already lost much of its savor. But there can be no serious doubt that for millions the Church *does* mean precisely that. It seems successful, but it is fundamentally unimportant because it is deemed to be marginal in its relevance. In so far as this is true, it is not only Church *members* but the *Church itself* which requires a radical conversion. Few phrases deserve currency in our time more than the phrase "The Conversion of the Church."

What we need to understand, in our generation, is that Christianity is a much bigger thing than we are wont to suppose. We are engaged in a big enterprise—the enterprise of changing the whole world. The real heresy is not some failure in some detail of theological belief, but that by which we trivialize the Christian undertaking. It is real tragedy to make it little when it ought to be big. It is a terrible sin to make people think the gospel is equivalent to the elimination of some minor vice or anything negative. A Christian, in Christ's sense, is not marked by the little habits which he has or does not have, but by his willingness to share in a radical undertaking of a change in men's hearts and a consequent change in human history. Our baptism is total or none.

What reason is there to suppose that our civilization, in contrast to civilizations which have preceded it, will endure? The person who has faced this question is hardly alive. That many different ways of life have flourished and have then declined is beyond contradiction. Consequently, there is no high probability that the fate of our civilization will be different—*unless.* The precise character of this "unless" is of such importance as to attract and to hold our best thinking both individually, and in groups. It is our most urgent question.

As we analyze the record of the experience of the past, we realize that neither technological nor material success is sufficient for endurance or even for survival. Life goes down, whatever the physical conditions may be, unless there is a relevant faith held by a sufficient number of the best minds. And not just any faith will suffice. It must have certain features, and it must be held with both intellectual integrity and dedication by self-conscious groups of people. Herein lies the crucial relevance of what we mean generally when we refer to the Church, since endurance requires both a spirit and a fellowship. Little is gained without the spirit, and the spirit cannot be maintained by separated individuals. Therefore the Church or something like it must be cherished, criticized, nourished, and reformed. The Church of Jesus Christ, with all its blemishes, its divisions, and its failures, remains our best hope of spiritual vitality. However poor it is, life without it is worse.

When a Christian expresses sadness about the Church, it is always the sadness of a lover. He knows that there have been great periods, and, consequently, he is not willing to settle for anything less than those in his own time. But, though he is saddened by the contrast between what now is and what has been, he is saddened even more by the contrast between all periods and what Christ evidently intended. Whatever else our Lord had in mind, it is clear that He envisioned something very big. He did not propose a slight change in an existing religion! The radical nature of the proposed Church is indicated by the fact that, in one chapter of the New Testament, Christ is reported three times as saying, "Something greater is here" (Matt. 12:6, 41, 42). A small venture would not have aroused such fierce opposition, but neither would it have been worth the trouble. The Christian Movement was initiated as the most radical of all revolutions!

Succeeding generations, as they try to evaluate our culture, will not have much evidence that is conclusive about our religious life, but they will have abundant evidence by which to judge our manner of living. What will surely strike researchers as odd if they still have access to the words of the Gospels is that these words will seem to have had no effect at all upon the manifest cult of self-indulgence. The remaining pages of slick and expensive advertising will appear more of a revelation than will the seemingly obsolete words of Christ about losing one's life and identification with the poor and humble.

It is hard to exaggerate the degree to which the modern Church seems irrelevant to modern man. The Church is looked upon as something to be neither seriously *fought* for, nor seriously *defended.* A church building is welcomed, partly because it provides such a nice place for a family wedding; and, after all, most families expect weddings, sooner or later. A church is also a good place to send the children on Sunday morning—they might learn something helpful, and certainly the experience of being sent will do them no harm. The point is that such conceptions are wholly consistent with the idea that the Church has only marginal relevance. We do not expect, for the most part, to find the gospel centered in a burning conviction which will make men and women change occupations, go to the ends of the earth, alter the practices of governments, redirect culture, and remake civilization.

Some indication of the mildness of our religious conviction is illustrated by the fact that we spend more on dog food than we spend on foreign missions. Another indication is the fact that we expect the inaugural address to be more inspiring than the prayers which precede and follow it. In short, we welcome religion, but we expect it to be innocuous and, above all, unfanatical. We are willing to accept it, provided that it involves no zeal. It is at this point that the contrast between the mildness of our faith and the burning devotion of the Communist faith is so disturbing. If only we possessed another object of devotion as an alternative to that involved in Christianity the situation might be less disturbing, but there is no such devotion in sight. Certainly democracy as an article of faith does not elicit any transforming power, while only a minority is able to understand the connection between democracy and a transforming faith which makes democracy reasonable.

True recovery is never a matter of going backward for the sake of re-establishing an older pattern, but rather of *uncovering* what has been hidden or overlaid and therefore forgotten. The purpose of such uncovering is the potential effect upon the present and the future. We go back to the New Testament, therefore, not as antiquarians and not as mere historians, but in the hope of finding hints of vitality of which our time is relatively unaware. We ought not, for example, to speak of recovering the lost provinces, if this means an attempt to return to the pattern of an earlier day, partly because this is an effort which never succeeds. We should speak, instead, of occupying the lost provinces in new and creative ways and of making spiritual strides which no previous generation has known or even imagined. Commitment is never real unless it leads to mission, and the mission of Christians is always one which points forward. If we are to go forward we must rid our minds of accepted ideas of what a true Church is, or ought to be, much as the research scientists of great industries, when they seek to make radical improvements, find it necessary to free their minds of current conceptions of what manufactured products should be like. In some industries, notably in the production of film, radical improvement has resulted from total reappraisal, which begins by a new hard look at the original experiment.

One of the most surprising facts about the early Church was its fundamental similarity to a military band. This is hard for us to recognize today because the ordinary successful church of the twentieth century is about as different from an army as anything we can imagine. Instead of being under anything resembling military discipline we pride ourselves on our "freedom." We go and come as we like, as no soldier can do; we give or withhold giving as we like; we serve when we get around to it. Obedience is considered an irrelevant notion, and the theme of "Onward Christian Soldiers" is so alien to our experience that some churches avoid the hymn entirely. A few avoid it on the mistaken assumption that it glorifies killing, which of course it does not. The military metaphor seems strained when it is applied to smartly dressed men and women riding in air-conditioned cars to air-conditioned "churches."

The earliest Christians owned no buildings at all, and with very good reason: they were so deeply engaged in the task of penetrating the world that they had no time to build a monument to themselves. The oldest known Christian structures—those underground at Rome—date from about A.D. 250. When Christians did finally begin to build, their major pattern was the dwelling house rather than the shrine. This was reasonable in view of the New Testament expression "the church in their house." There is nothing wrong with beauty, and we may be truly gratified for the labor which has gone into some ecclesiastical buildings, such as the medieval cathedrals, but we must never let even their beauty cause us to forget what the main purpose of a Christian building is. What we can say with real confidence is that a building designed to be used only once or twice a week is wholly inadequate. We need spiritual laboratories, with all of the emphasis placed on simple beauty and daily function rather than upon ostentation, or display. We have made a great start when we see the church building not as a holy place, but as the headquarters of the company, from which the recruits are expected to go *out*.

The idea of the Church as a military company was by no means strange to early Christians. Indeed, military language can be found in various parts of the New Testament. It need hardly be said that this language had no reference to killing, or preparation for destruction, but rather to the mood of men and women whose responsibilities were of the same demanding character as those of enlisted persons. Thus it seems wholly natural to read of "Epaphroditus my brother and fellow worker and fellow soldier" (Philippians 2:25); of "a good soldier of Christ Jesus," with his share of suffering (II Timothy 2:3); of "Archippus our fellow soldier" (Philemon 2); of "the whole armor of God" (Ephesians 6:11). It is perfectly clear that early Christians considered

Christ their Commander-in-Chief, that they were in a company of danger which involved great demands upon their lives, and that to be a Christian was to be engaged in Christ's service. It cannot be too emphatically pointed out that such "service" was not remotely similar to what we call a "service" today, a polite gathering of auditors, sitting in comfortable pews listening to a clergyman and a choir.

The Church cannot fulfill its sacred vocation unless it is a penetrating force, as salt is, and the penetration cannot even begin unless the fellowship which is in the Church has something of the character of an explosion. Little can be done with a smoldering fire; somehow there must be a blaze. But how is this to be achieved? We do not know all of the answers to this practical question, but we know something. Since the starter of the fire is Christ Himself, our initial means of achieving a real blaze is that of confronting Him as steadily and as directly as is humanly possible. When the closeness to Christ is lost, the fire either goes out or it merely smolders, like the fires in the great swamps which are hidden from the sun. A Christianity which ceases to be Christ-centered may have some other valuable features, but it is usually lacking in power.

At the very time when we are beginning to realize how formidable are the forces arrayed against Christianity in the modern world, an old yet new conception of the fellowship of those enlisted in Christ's cause is re-emerging. This may be one of the times when the greatness of the need may be matched by the vitality of the response. There is no real hope of such vitality unless and until we understand what Christian enlistment means. Because the trouble we face is more serious than we ordinarily suppose, the solution of our problems will likewise lie along deeper lines than those to which we are accustomed.

Evangelism occurs when people are so enkindled by contact with the central fire of Christ that they, in turn, set others on fire. The only adequate evidence that anything is on fire is the pragmatic evidence that other fires are started by it. A fire that does not spread must eventually go out! This is the point of Emil Brunner's dictum that "the Church exists by mission as fire exists by burning." A person who claims to have a religious experience, yet makes no effort to share or to extend it, has not really entered into Christ's Company at all. In short, an unevangelistic or unmissionary Christianity is a contradiction in terms. If we did not know this by other means we should know it by pondering Christ's statement of his incendiary purpose.

We shall not be saved by anything less than commitment, and the commitment will not be effective unless it finds expression in a committed fellowship. If we have any knowledge of human nature, we begin by rejecting the arrogance of self-sufficiency. Committed men need the fellowship not because they are strong, but because they are—and know that they are—fundamentally sinful and weak.

It is generally recognized that though commitment is of the first importance, men may have more than one object of their commitment. The full commitment of millions of Germans, prior to and during the Great War, was to Adolf Hitler and *his* cause. Other millions are today committed to Marxism. That is why it is now recognized that Marxian communism is fundamentally a religion rather than a mere economic or political system. The fact that it denies God does not keep it from being religious. Christians have no monopoly on commitment; they simply have a different object. A Christian is a person who confesses that, amidst the manifold and confusing voices heard in the world, there is one Voice which supremely wins his full assent, uniting all his powers, intellectual and emotional, into a single pattern of self-giving. That Voice is Jesus Christ. A Christian not only believes *that* He was; he believes *in Him* with all his heart and strength and mind. Christ appears to the Christian as the one stable point or fulcrum in all the relativities of history. Once the Christian has made this primary commitment he still has perplexities, but he begins to know the joy of being used for a mighty purpose, by which his little life is dignified.

Though the word is shocking to modern man, there is a valid sense in which the Christian Movement must be envisaged as a *violent* one. It is violent because of the enormous break in the conception of what true religion involves. It would not be violent to have slightly better priests, or purified temple practices, or improved synagogue services. Even what John did at the Jordan was really part of the old order, antecedent to the revolution, but not a part of it. "The law and the prophets were until John; since then the good news of the kingdom of God is preached, and every one enters it violently" (Luke 16:16). We shall never have a real renewal of the Church without a serious grappling with this shocking expression. The deepest danger facing the Church is that it may remain pre-Christian. We need all of the help we can get from one another in order to try to understand what it means to enter the Kingdom "violently."

If we realize that Christ was organizing a genuine "company" many points immediately become clear. Herein is the significance of the cryptic "Follow me." He was not advising people to go to church, or even to attend the synagogue; He was, instead, asking for recruits in a company of danger. He was not asking primarily for belief, but for commitment with subsequent involvement. It is significant that the first of those who answered this call to enlistment followed Him before they knew who He was. The recognition of Christ's true character, in Matthew 16, comes long after the successful appeal of Matthew 4:19. The well-known words are far more understandable if we see them as the call of a recruiting officer, "And he said to them, 'Follow me, and I will make you fishers of men.' Immediately they left their nets and followed him."

We are made to be spent. This is inherent in the very nature of the human situation. The revolting symbol of the yoke, feared and rejected by many Christians even to this day, comes to stand for the chief meaning of the Christian life. What is a Christian? A Christian is one who seeks, in spite of his failures, to wear Christ's yoke with Him. This is not the conclusion of the gospel, but it is a big step on the way. It takes a great deal of thinking to understand in detail what the wearing of the yoke must mean, but at least we know where to start. There is something better than comfort, and there is something better than disturbance. As we try to wear Christ's yoke with Him, we begin to learn what it is.

We all understand, when we give our minds carefully to the question, that to be an effective Christian it is not enough to be an individual believer. Inadequate as the fellowship of the Church may be, in many generations, including our own, there is not the slightest chance of Christian vitality without it. Apart from the poor and all too human fellowship called the Church we should not have had even the New Testament. Men are often brave and good alone, but they are never really effective unless they share in some kind of group reality. Voices crying in the wilderness are not permanently recorded. Furthermore, the indispensability of the Church is demonstrated by the fact that the new life normally arises from the inside. The ultimate evidence of the divine ordering of the Church is the way in which it is always the members of the Church itself who are the most intelligent critics of her life and witness.

The crucial question today is not whether we must have a fellowship, for on that point we are reasonably clear; the crucial question concerns the *character* of the fellowship.

The more we think about it the more we realize that it must be a fellowship of the committed. This is because mere belief is never enough. Some writers and speakers give the impression that the main adversary we face is atheism, with the consequence that they try to convince other men that "there is a God." Although the philosophy of religion, including the case for theistic realism, is an important intellectual discipline and one which a true scholar will never neglect or even minimize, the chief barrier to a renewed vitality in the Christian society is not lack of belief. Millions who feel no sense of urgency about the Christian endeavor will list themselves, when inquiry is made, as believers of some sort.

We cannot understand the idea of a company apart from the concept of *involvement*. What we seek is not a fellowship of the righteous or of the self-righteous, but rather a fellowship of men and women who, though they recognize that they are inadequate, nevertheless can be personally involved in the effort to make Christ's kingdom prevail. Perhaps the greatest single weakness of the contemporary Christian Church is that millions of supposed members are not really involved at all and, what is worse, do not think it strange that they are not. As soon as we recognize Christ's intention to make His Church a militant company we understand at once that the conventional arrangement cannot suffice. There is no real chance of victory in a campaign if ninety per cent of the soldiers are untrained and uninvolved, but that is exactly where we stand now. Most alleged Christians do not now understand that loyalty to Christ means sharing personally in His ministry, going or staying as the situation requires.

Each of us is bound to die, and every rational person is highly conscious that his life is short, but there need be no tragedy in this. It is surely not so bad to die, providing one has really lived *before* he dies. Life need not be long to be good, for indeed it cannot be long. The tragedy is not that all die, but that so many fail really to live. The chief way in which men miss much of the possible richness of living is by playing the game safely, seeking always to avoid all risk. The problem of every man is how he will sell his life and, if he is wise, he will sell it high. But this is not possible except in terms of a wager. The best life is one in which, committed to some cause which has won our full loyalty, we give ourselves and all our energies to it in uncalculating and unmercenary devotion. Such lives have actually been lived, and, when we see them, we know that they are good.

The nature of a true Christian society or Church is so rich that it cannot be fully expressed in a single idea. Love is not the only mark—it is merely the final mark. Though the marks of the true Church are many, a particular mark may, with logical consistency, be recognized as more important than the others. When we truly become a Company of Christ's Committed Ones we exhibit a number of features which fit together into a total complex of greater and lesser features. In such a society there is *commitment,* and *enlistment,* and *witness,* and *penetration* of common life, and *caring,* but the greatest of these is *caring.* The Church of Jesus Christ is not merely a society of love, for love is conceivable in any historical tradition, but if the Church is genuine, it must always involve love as the most important single attribute.

Though there is no need at this point to essay a full description of a committed Christianity, it may be said briefly that what is meant is a faith marked by a burning conviction and the consequent desire to see it spread. It is the exact opposite of mild religion with its easy tolerance. Committed Christianity is radically different from "religion in general," being based on a conviction which is definite. In the most profound sense of the word it is "narrow" and it is unapologetically so. A Christian is committed to the conviction that God really is, that He is wholly personal, that He is like Jesus Christ, and that God has a particular interest in each individual of the human race. We do not deny that there are good people who reject every item of the faith just mentioned. What we affirm is that this is what Christianity is. The person who claims to be a Christian while rejecting such convictions is simply engaging in a contradiction of terms. That the Christian Way is intrinsically narrow is the clear affirmation of part of the Sermon on the Mount: "For the gate is narrow and the way is hard, that leads to life, and those who find it are few" (Matt. 7:14).

Selections in Chapter One are taken from:
The Incendiary Fellowship
Alternative to Futility
The Yoke of Christ
The Company of the Committed
The Life We Prize

Chapter Two

A CHRIST-CENTERED FAITH

A Christian is one who believes that the teachings of Jesus Christ are the only sure, solid form of ideology in this world of conflicting philosophies. In a culture where every new wind of doctrine tosses us to and fro, Elton Trueblood helps his readers to clarify their thinking on the importance of keeping Christ as the focal point of their faith, and by so doing he is able to give them a place to stand. Religion in general, Dr. Trueblood believes, is a weak substitute for a Christ-centered faith of commitment, and only as Christians come to this important truth will they be changed persons, and thus enabled to go out and change others.

J.R.N.

What is a Christian? A Christian is a person who has fallen in love with Jesus Christ and who is, consequently, willing to witness to that love and to try to demonstrate it, as Christ's emissary, to all the rest of God's children. It is not cold detachment. It is not looking at the gospel and saying, "That is an interesting idea." Such an approach, whatever the field of inquiry, doesn't get us anywhere at all. Life is a great mystery at best; it is the sort of thing that is never penetrated apart from passion. A Christian is one who looks at the life of Christ and who is so moved by it that he says, "I love Thee, Lord Jesus. Come into my heart, come in today; come in to stay."

A Christian is a person who, with all the honesty of which he is capable, becomes convinced that the fact of Jesus Christ is the most trustworthy that he knows in his entire universe of discourse. Christ thus becomes both his central postulate and the Archimedean fulcrum which, because it is really firm, enables him to operate with confidence in other areas.

"Meditate on His life," wrote à Kempis, "and thou wilt be ashamed to find how far removed thou art from His perfection." Real confrontation should involve all that is needed in devotional experience. It should emphasize both our unworthiness and our hope, both our separation from God and our potential reconciliation. It is almost impossible to confront Christ without consequent prayer, and the experience is not likely to be long continued without real amendment of life.

The present sickness of civilization, of which we are so acutely conscious, is marked by many disturbing symptoms, but none is more disturbing than the present condition of religious faith. Our time cannot be accurately described as a time of irreligion, but rather as one in which we see the alarming growth of what we are forced to recognize as false religions. The most conspicuous of these involve fanatical devotion to living men, whose unworthiness is obvious to any detached observer. It is an elementary, though often neglected observation on the history of religions, that religion may be extremely harmful as well as beneficial, both to its adherents and to the human race generally. There are bad religions, especially those based on falsehood, and we are deluged with them now.

For a number of reasons the basic faiths, which have done so much to provide a cultural unity to the western world for centuries, have been undermined, and countless people, thus unsettled, have become easy marks for the propagation of new faiths. It has been demonstrated, once more, that the house which is swept and garnished cannot long remain empty.

The closest historical parallel is to be found in the breakup of antique civilization, when men, having ceased to believe in the objective reality of the pagan gods and goddesses, and having experienced what has been termed a "loss of nerve," were adopting new faiths. Then, as now, they turned, on the other hand, to emperor worship, with its attendant persecutions, and, on the other hand, to pseudo-mysticism, with its interest in self-culture.

Into the antique civilization there came a message of life and power teaching men to think of the one true God as objectively real, far above all particular men and particular nations, and declaring that men had been granted, and were still granted, direct knowledge of the divine nature. This message turned confusion into order, becoming the central element in a unifying pattern of existence.

It is now abundantly clear to thoughtful persons that the sickness of our civilization requires the vigorous reintroduction of some such central faith. A thorough-going faith in God who is at once universal in sovereignty, spiritual in nature, and Christlike in character, would make the bizaare and sectional religions of our day impossible. Such a faith would give men incentive without hatred and confidence without bombast. It would provide an effective antidote for inflated nationalism and, at the same time, lead men and women to take seriously their responsibilities to their fellow-men, inasmuch as all are children of the same Father. Since the predicament of paganism can hardly fail to be increasingly acute, there is excellent reason to suppose that nothing short of a general return to the Christian faith can counterbalance the disruptive and centrifugal forces of modern life.

If God is, indeed, truly personal, as so much of experience indicates, we should expect that His most vivid revelation would necessarily be a personal one. The complete way in which He could be shown to us would not be in the majesty of mountains or in the wonder of the stars or even in the intricacy of a cell, but only in a personal life, sharing, as do our lives, in both affection and temptation, yet perfect where we are imperfect. The good news is that this has occurred! All other historical persons can be approached or forgotten at will, but there lived One whom men cannot leave alone. He revealed the truth of God and man, not merely by what he taught, but far more by what he did, and above all, by what he *was*.

It is a hopeful fact that, when a truly God-inspired man lives, anywhere, there seems to be a general recognition of that tremendous fact. There have been, in many different traditions, great personalities, universally respected, and for these we are grateful. Many have made a divine witness and thereby a genuine revelation. Each of those who has won universal respect, from Buddha and Confucius and Moses to Gandhi and Schweitzer in our own day, has helped us to understand what God is. But there is One who, through centuries and in all cultures, has revealed God supremely. In the person of Christ, God is made understandable to man. Much as we admire the great teachers, when we approach reverently the life and death of Jesus, the knowledge slowly dawns upon us that here we are in the presence of something radically different. The great teachers have explored the world and their own hearts and, as a consequence, have given flashes of almost incredible genius, but with Jesus, however we may resist the conviction, we find something other than genius. He comes, not as a Seeker, but rather as a Revealer who tells us what He knows, not what he has deduced. What others do partially He does completely. Imperfect as was the understanding of his reporters, and much as they were bound by the limitations of the thought forms of their day, nevertheless the gospels preserve enough of the stupendous truth to leave us humble in His presence. Much must have been lost, but much remains and what remains is sufficient to shake any man's complacency, if he will submit his mind humbly to the story. The more often we read the story the more sure we are that men are right in dating all events from the birth of Jesus.

For the Christian, Christ is not the end of the quest; He is the beginning. Starting with Him, we are forced by intellectual integrity to proceed a long way. If we are committed to Him, we trust Him about the being and the character of God, about the reality of prayer, about the possibility of miracle, and about the life everlasting. The deepest conviction of the Christian is that Christ was not wrong! Particularly, we are convinced that He was not wrong in His report about Himself. It is important to remember that our commitment is to one who said, "All things have been delivered to me by my Father; and no one knows the Father except the Son and any one to whom the Son chooses to reveal him" (Matt. 11:27).

To say that Christ is the fulcrum is not merely to say that He was the greatest figure of history or the finest moral teacher. It is, instead, to see Him as the genuine revelation of the mystery of existence, the one clear light among the many shadows. Commitment is thus vastly more than mere admiration. It means passionate involvement in His life, teachings, death, and resurrection. It is to share with Him when He says, "I am the resurrection and the life" (John 11:25). We are not Christians until we are committed, and we are not committed until we combine, in our faith in Christ, the reasons of the heart with the reasons of the intellect. Commitment to Christ does not solve our problems; on the contrary, it adds new ones. Often it brings not peace but a sword (Matt. 10:34), because it produces a holy disturbance. In any case, it destroys what is ordinarily understood as peace of mind. Like Archimedes, we still have to do the work of lifting, but we have a solid point from which to operate.

One way in which freshness may be achieved in the contemporary situation is by helping people to ask new questions. To many the question of the divinity of Christ seems stale and boring, but often these same people can become genuinely interested when they are involved in a radically different approach. This different approach, which stresses the Christ-likeness of God, has an immense intellectual appeal because it enables men to move from the relatively known to the relatively unknown, the freshness of the approach lying as much in the question as in the answer. The question becomes, "What is God like?" Is God a mere impersonal force? Is God merely a Ground of Being? Is God vindictive and uncaring? Or is God like Jesus Christ? Jesus Himself answers this last question in the affirmative, and if it is a true answer it is the most exciting news in all the world. A Christian, however imperfect he may be, is a believer, and *this* is what he believes.

The most pragmatic of reasons for seeing that Christ is the most dependable of realities is that of changed human lives. When we consider Saul of Tarsus on the road to Damascus, we are in the realm of the empirical as contrasted with the merely speculative. Saul said it was the Living Christ who had met him, and the person who seeks to deny this is confronted with the fact of a permanent change in Saul's character. We cannot, of course, know whether a man is lying when he says "I believe," because belief is intrinsically internal and personal, but the evidence of changed lives is something which other people can observe. In Saul's case the change was so radical that it led to the production of some of the finest literature of the world, a literature which would not have been produced apart from the crucial encounter.

The evidence of lives changed by contact with Christ is so abundant that the full story can never be told; it is, indeed, of a kind not matched anywhere in any culture. The changed lives have come about, not primarily by a set of ideas or by acceptance of a doctrine, but by commitment to a Person. Long after the time of the Apostle Paul a man named Francis, who lived in Assisi, exhibited a change so great that he in turn mightily affected others.

The Christian takes his stand on the fact that lives can be made new by fellowship with Christ, and he does not know of any other source of change and renewal which is equal to this . . . We have learned that a mere inner direction, no matter how frantic or obsessive, is not sufficient for the new life we sorely need, for we do not have the power to save ourselves. My own life cannot be unified except by that to which I am devoted. But where shall I turn? A mere "ism" will never suffice. Because persons are superior, in kind, not only to all *things* but even to all *ideas*, I need a person to whom I can give myself and thereby find myself. But not just any person will suffice; it must be a person commitment to whom can change the imperfect world order.

We may consider turning to Karl Marx, but his is not a sufficiently revolutionary mentality. Because we are dulled by familiarity we forget, sometimes, that Christ provides the most revolutionary of conceptions, in that He sees each individual as an unconditional object of the divine Concern. This undermines all racism and, when taken seriously, provides an antidote to all injustice.

We speak only with tremendous reticence about the "mind of God," but we can speak with some confidence about the mind of Christ. Never should we cease to be thankful for the production and preservation of the four Gospels. In spite of the welcome scientific study of historical and literary origins, they stand up remarkably under full and sustained examination. Though New Testament scholarship has made great advances, there is no good reason why the ordinary Christian should be intimidated by the confident assertions of men who claim to know definitely which parts of the Gospel record are original and which were added as a result of the needs and experience of the early Church. The person who claims to be able to say, with certitude, which of the Gospel passages are authentic utterances of Christ and which are not, is claiming more than any man actually knows. It is important to remember that the new knowledge of the flesh-and-blood Christ is something we owe to the Church. It is not true, therefore, as is sometimes said, that the early Church was interested only in the Eternal or risen Lord. There is little doubt that the chief incentive for the production of accounts of what Christ did and said and suffered was that early Christians, many of whom were Greek, desired to know the objective and historical truth about His appearing. The Gospels were the response of those who knew.

The early Christian desire for the production of Gospels is an important revelation. The members of the early Church wanted to know more about Christ because they believed that He was the image of God the Father. They could find out very little by any direct means of encounter with God, but they believed that they could learn a great deal by encountering Him indirectly, through Christ. Their tremendous affirmation, which underlies all they did and said and which is the secret of their boldness, was that though they could not see God they could see His *image*, and they wanted to learn more about that image. It was because they believed that Christ was more than Teacher that they wanted to know the details of His teaching. Early Christians preserved the record of the teachings of Christ because they were convinced that He was not merely a teacher. Only on this hypothesis can we account for the fact that they went to so much trouble. They took great pains to know Christ because, facing the fact of His life, they had concluded that he was indeed the very brightness of God's own glory and "the express image of God's person" (Heb. 1:3, A.V.).

Though it was once fashionable to make a sharp distinction between the historic Christ and the Living Christ, it is no longer so. What we see is that this sharp distinction cannot be meaningfully made, because in both cases we are dealing with the same reality. Since Christ can be our Teacher as truly today as He was the Teacher of the apostles by the Sea of Galilee, it is blasphemous to speak of Him merely in the past tense. Tremendous excitement is involved in the idea that Christ can be known in the present tense, and that He can be known in the most mundane events. When we speak of the Living Christ we do not mean the same as when we refer to the "spirit of Abraham Lincoln," which is another matter altogether. We mean, in reference to the Living Christ, that Christ is a Person who is still alive in very fact, and not metaphorically. Only the naïve would suppose that this living reality is a matter of flesh. But what good reason is there, after all, to suppose that fleshly existence is the only form of existence?

When we speak of the Living Christ we do not refer to the reserved sacrament. Christ, as we know Him now, is not something which can be carried about in a box and adored. The Real Presence is never confined to an altar, and, indeed, has no connection with any magic at all. The doctrine of the real presence is simply a way of affirming the fact that humble men and women who are neither insane nor stupid find that He is with them on life's darkest as well as its brightest ways. Because Christ is alive, He is not limited to one area or one historic period. Though He was in Galilee, He is not confined to Galilee. Fortunately, neither is He confined to the West, nor identified with it.

One of the finest fruits of Christian revelation is the way in which it makes world religions allies rather than competitors. Christ came, He said, not to destroy but to fulfill. Anything valuable in Buddhism or Hinduism or Islam we can therefore honor and employ, for Christ has "other sheep, that are not of this fold" (John 10:16). The spirit of this important insight is caught in the prologue of the Letter to the Hebrews, "In many and various ways God spoke of old." All the insights of the Hebrew prophets are ennobled by the new context which Christ provides. The effect of this on missionary work is crucial, for the wise missionary, rather than being the servant or exponent of Western civilization, is instead the messenger of Christ. Although, if he is a mature thinker, he knows that the redemptive fellowship is important, he does not feel it necessary to defend the Church. Instead of being the servant of Christianity, he is an apostle of Christ. This is possible because Christ, far from being an item of our culture, belongs in reality to all cultures, and is the Judge of all, including our own.

Why hold to Christ? What is there about Him which convinces us that He provides the one firm ground mortal men can know? This question has always been asked, but because of widespread interest in, and some knowledge of, world religions, it is being asked with renewed insistence today. Admitting that He made extreme claims, what reason (we ask ourselves in our insistent dialogue) is there to suppose that Christ's claims have any justification?

It is popular in some circles to accept Christ as a teacher, but not as one who provides a unique revelation of the Father. The familiar stance is one that involves admiring comments about Christ but denies any supernaturalism. Such a position, however, cannot be defended rationally, since all four Gospels bristle with supernatural claims on the part of Jesus. The person who takes this position has surely not read the Gospels! Familiarity has blinded men to the radical nature of Christ's claims about His peculiar relationship to the Father. Both C. S. Lewis and J. B. Phillips have performed a useful service in helping readers to see that the only alternative to acceptance of Christ's teaching about Himself is that He was either "a lunatic or a quack." The inescapable conclusion is that, if Christ was only a teacher, He was a very misleading teacher.

Ought we to pray alone or with others? Here both the teaching and practice of Christ provide a clear answer. There are times, and perhaps a majority of times, when we ought to pray alone. Christ's practice in this regard is well represented in the New Testament. In the Garden of Gesthemane He prayed alone, even though the apostles were not far distant (Luke 22:41). We know that He went apart to pray in the early morning hours (Mark 1:35). Further, in the Sermon on the Mount, as a clear alternative to the kind of prayer which may be public because it is really ostentatious, He said, "When you pray, go into your room and shut the door and pray to your Father who is in secret" (Matt. 6:6).

Some people have been so impressed by Christ's advice about solitary prayer that they have drawn the wrong conclusion that prayer ought never to be experienced in company with others. But Christ supported both solitary and group experience and exemplified both; they are not, of course, mutually exclusive. The experience on the Mountain of Transfiguration was clearly that of a prayer group (Mark 9:2). Moreover, the moving statement about the presence in the midst is itself an affirmation of the value and necessity of prayer with others. We reach a deep place, indeed, when we hear Christ say, "For where two or three are gathered in my name, there am I in the midst of them" (Matt. 18:20). The most unequivocal promise is made, not concerning the prayer of one, but the prayer of two (Matt. 18:19). The conclusion we must reach is that there is a time to pray alone, and likewise a time to pray with others. What is odd is the idea that it is necessary to choose.

For Christ, and for all Christians, belief in continued life following death is clearly a corollary of belief in God. The final belief in the Apostles' Creed comes last, because it is a consequence. If God is not, then there is no reason to believe in the continued existence of finite persons and the subject is not really worth discussing. If God is not, spiritual experience on our planet is a totally unexplained aberration, with no assignable cause, and there is no reason to expect its continuation after the body has died. If God is not, Lord Bertrand Russell is right when he says that all the monuments of man's genius will be "buried beneath the debris of a universe in ruins." But if God really is, as Christ both believed and revealed, then there is nothing strange at all about the continued existence of those who are the special objects of the Father's care. The oddity would be cessation of existence, since that would mean that God either will not or cannot keep alive the individuals whose lives He prizes.

It must be understood that the life everlasting, as affirmed by Christians, and as expressed in the entire New Testament, is unequivocally personal and individual. There is nothing said about the individual spirit returning to God and being lost as a drop of water loses its identity when it returns to the ocean. It is not the mass of humanity, or some abstract deposit of spirit, that is supremely valued, but rather the individual person, for it is in the principle of individuality that value resides. Not sparrows in general, but the individual sparrow is the object of the Father's care. "Not one of them is forgotten before God" (Luke 12:6). Though spirit in general is a mere abstraction, individual spirit is concrete, and God, as represented by Christ, values the concrete. We do not and probably cannot know the details of the life to come, but we are assured that it will be a conscious existence, marked by a true liberation from many of the limitations we suffer in our brief period of preparation on this earth.

The conviction of the earliest Christians was that they were, indeed, the children of the resurrection, and this seems to have provided the most powerful motivation in their total lives. Since they were engaged, they thought, not merely in a temporary earthly struggle, but in an eternal undertaking, every event was thereby potentially glorified. In writing of this conviction the Apostle Paul, who did not claim to be a good speaker, but was undoubtedly a most gifted writer, rose to heights of eloquence. Of the Living Christ he said that his own central purpose was "that I may know him and the power of his resurrection, and may share his sufferings, becoming like him in his death, that if possible I may attain the resurrection from the dead" (Phil. 3:10, 11). It was because this faith was more than mere speculation that it was so evidently marked by power.

The entire mood of the early Christians, in reference to survival beyond the grave, was marked by a combination of confidence and severest agnosticism. They did not allow their confidence, which was complete, to drive them into a position in which they claimed to know more than had been given them. Perhaps the most beautiful expression of this combined mood is one sentence in John's First Letter: "Beloved, we are God's children now; it does not yet appear what we shall be, but we know that when he appears we shall be like him, for we shall see him as he is" (I John 3:2). John Greenleaf Whittier was writing in conscious association with this humble mood when, disclaiming any detailed knowledge, he reported that he was "Assured alone that life and death, His mercy underlies." In the new life that is waiting for the sons of the resurrection there will be nothing to disappoint, though there may be much to surprise.

In my own life, I certainly began as a skeptic so far as the resurrection of Christ is concerned. I thought of the story as comparable to stories in Greek mythology, and accordingly carried my doubt to the point of denial. I knew, of course, that the early Christians believed that Christ rose, but I was aware of the fact that many people, in many ages, have believed things that are manifestly untrue. The first real change in my conclusion came when I began to consider seriously a particular kind of evidence, that of altered lives. Suddenly I saw that the primary evidence provided by the apostles is not what they *said*, but what they *became*.

At one point in time the erstwhile followers of Christ were a poor little bedraggled band; they were going home because the dream had evaporated. They had believed that, somehow, Christ was the herald of a new order, but now it was evident that they had been wrong in this judgment, since He had been killed just like any criminal. They were, of course, well aware of the stories of other leaders whose work suddenly came to nothing. "For before these days," said Gamaliel, "Theudas arose, giving himself out to be somebody, and a number of men, about four hundred, joined him; but he was slain and all who followed him were dispersed and came to nothing" (Acts 5:36).

It looked, in that bleak time, as though the same pathetic tragedy had been reenacted. What is more poignant than the remark of the disappointed apostles, "We had hoped that he was one to redeem Israel" (Luke 24:21)? The enthusiasm of His presence, the shared vitality, the creative hope—all these were gone, and one more bubble had burst. But then another event, and one of a totally different order, began to occur. In a short time these broken men became strong, confident, and bold as lions. They sang; they rejoiced; they healed; they taught; they suffered triumphantly. And this they did, not only for a few days of passing enthusiasm, but for all the remainder of their lives. They had faced persecution and even death with a triumphant spirit that baffled their tormentors. A characteristic account is the following: "So they took his advice, and when they had called in the apostles, they beat them and charged them not to speak in the name of Jesus, and let them go. Then they left the presence of the council, rejoicing that they were counted worthy to suffer dishonor for the name. And every day in the temple and at home they did not cease teaching and preaching Jesus as the Christ" (Acts 5:40-42).

Now the serious student must seek an explanation for a change so revolutionary and so enduring. What was the sufficient cause? To this the early Christians gave their own answer: *it happened, they asserted, solely because Christ arose from the dead.* He talked with them, so that their hearts burned within them. Since the best evidence is found in consequences rather than in mere words, it is hard to think of events in ancient history for which the verification is more compelling.

The idea that our earthly bodies, which are made of flesh, will continue to exist eternally, is so preposterous that reverent believers have regularly rejected it. One reason why it is preposterous is that such a continuation would perpetuate rather than correct the injustices of this life. For the hunchback to be eternally a hunchback would be a mark, not of heaven, but of hell! Only if such inequities are transcended can the redeeming love of Christ be exemplified.

Thinking people ought to be neither surprised nor puzzled to learn that, when Christians refer to the resurrection of their bodies, they are employing a figure of speech. No one supposed that, when Christ says that He is the Door, He is made of *wood*. The truth is that the deepest truths cannot be communicated except in figures. While the term "body" is manifestly inadequate in reference to the future life, it is reasonable for us to employ it, because any alternative we can think of is *less* adequate. But when we use it we have a responsibility to explain it, so as to reduce confusion as far as possible.

The point to which we must return again and again is

that, in our conviction that the decay of the flesh is not a final event, we must meticulously avoid reference to a vague spirituality. There may be in store for us something better than what we know of personality, but we may be assured that this new life will at least be personal. Though we know that "we shall be changed," we have good reason to suppose that the love of Christ will not change and that it will dignify our little lives, however different they may be from anything we now experience. Now we see through a glass, darkly, but then we shall see face to face. In this life we are forced to live by faith; in the life to come we shall live, not by faith, but by open vision.

There is no way in which we can exaggerate the supporting evidence of the central conviction that what Christ taught is true and that His continuing presence is a reality. He appears to some people in solitude, but more commonly He appears to men and women in the fellowship. Imperfect as the Church is, and has always been, the central verifying experience is that "where two or three are gathered in my name, there am I in the midst of them" (Matt. 18:20).

Selections in Chapter Two are taken from:
  The Yoke of Christ
  A Place to Stand
  Confronting Christ
  The Trustworthiness of Religious Experience
  The Life We Prize
  The Validity of the Christian Mission

Chapter
Three

WHOLISTIC CHRISTIANITY

O ne of the cornerstones of Elton Trueblood's thinking has been his belief in the "third way." In a world of "either-or" choices, Dr. Trueblood challenges his readers to pursue the course of "both-and" in the life of religious faith. A Christian is one who practices an inner life of devotion, but he must also be committed to an outer life of service and a life of Christian study, if his faith is to be genuine. In this chapter the vision of wholeness is presented in a way that challenges the traditional misconceptions of having to choose between any of these different emphases of the Gospel, when the option of a combination is available, and is, in fact, much more desirable in the life of faith.

J.R.N.

Is the Christian a person who loves God, or is he one who loves his fellow men? Though the question is asked, it is really a foolish one. A Christian is one who is committed to Christ, and Christ stressed the two commandments without preference. Though there are many paradoxes in the Gospels, and though its truth cannot be rightly stated apart from paradox, there is no paradox more striking than that of the "double priority." Christ gave two "firsts." The one "first" was exactly what His hearers expected, because they were familiar with the Shema (Deut. 6:4), which was repeated daily. They knew that they were required to love God and to love Him wholly.

The other "first," which in the teaching of Christ is of equal standing, is the requirement that the disciple should love his neighbor as *himself* (Lev. 19:18). The Christian, accordingly, is convinced that there can be no adequate faith that does not recognize and encourage this double priority. A Christian is asked to include in his life both piety and service. Then he can hold the roots and the fruits of his faith in one organic content. Each needs the other.

We live in a time of greatness. There is evidence of greatness even in our recognition of the enormity and complexity of our human problems. "The greatness of man is great," said Blaise Pascal over three hundred years ago, "in that he knows himself to be miserable." But this is by no means the end of the story. No one in his senses can doubt the greatness of the achievement of the Apollo flights. Possibly the most encouraging feature of the first moon landing, more carefully observed than any other event in all previous history, has been the way in which it has led to reverence. There seemed, on that day, to be a complete absence of conceit as the most sophisticated observers expressed their reverence unabashedly. This is a good sign. At his best moments, man is reverent, as well as compassionate and intelligent. That the vision of wholeness is still appealing is, in every way, a sign of hope and an indication of what is possible in the future. An important ministry, therefore, is the ministry of encouragement to those who are dissatisfied with the division that they observe, though they may be doubtful about the way to turn.

The new man for our time is the whole man, the man who consciously rejects the temptation to limit himself to one part of a totality, when such limitation is not required. But where is the inspiration to wholeness to be found? It is certainly not found in science. The truth is that it is most likely to be found in the Christian faith. Though it is sorrowfully true that some of the worst fragmentation is currently demonstrated in the Christian community itself, the Christian faith, particularly through its Founder and its Scriptures, possesses resources for the transcendence of one-sidedness. By the miracle of the preservation of the Gospels, Christians have a marvelous antidote to divisiveness of every kind. If they will study the Gospels directly, and not merely study *about* them, they will find in them the fairest presentation of wholeness that the human race has known. There is found One who weeps and One who laughs, and only the foolish suppose that there is any incompatibility between these two expressions of the divine character. There is found equal emphasis upon the life of devotion and the life of action. Only the obtuse can fail to see that Christ both healed and prayed, and that in His judgment the former could not be achieved without the latter (Mark 9:29).

What is becoming increasingly clear is that the major tragedy of the new separatism emerges because each party is deprived of something that it needs, and something that the opposite party has to offer. The pietist needs action and the activist needs piety. Each is a half man, made such by an unnecessary act of self-limitation and consequent impoverishment. The really wonderful fact is that a number of

Christian leaders are now keenly aware of this, and are, consequently, trying to develop the new image that the life of our times requires. The best leaders are both service-centered and Christ-centered.

It is time now to take a further step and to show that the new man who is to be truly contemporary must include, not just two, but three elements in the totality of his faith. These three are like three legs of a stool, the smallest number possible if the stool is to stand upright. The three necessary elements in any genuine Christianity are, first, the experience of inner vitality that comes by the life of prayer, second, the experience of outer action in which the Christian carries on a healing ministry, both to individuals and to social institutions, and third, the experience of care-ful thinking by which the credibility of the entire operation may be supported. Religions tend to die when any one of the three is omitted for an extended period of time.

The Christian faith must rediscover its own essential genius, which is the union of the secular and the sacred, of matter and of spirit, the common and the divine. If the Christian Church is to regain its hold on the life of modern man it must find ways of meeting people where their inter-ests lie, and this requires disciplined imagination. We have to *think*, if we are to know how to do it. The task of those who feel a sense of responsibility for the work of the Church is not to condemn the present lack of spirituality nor to wring their hands over the wickedness of the con-temporary world, but to be on the lookout for the meaning already inherent in the life men now know, and to find ways of enhancing this meaning by lifting it up into a con-text of divine love.

The differences in human life depend, for the most part, not on what men *do*, but upon the meaning and purpose of their acts. All are *born*, all *die*, all *lose their loved ones*, nearly all *marry* and nearly all *work*, but the *significance* of these acts may vary enormously. The same physical act may be in one situation vulgar and in another holy. The same work may be elevating or degrading. The major question is not, "What act do I perform?" but "In what frame do I put it?" Wisdom about life consists in taking the inevitable ventures which are the very stuff of common existence, and glorifying them.

Shall we stress words or deeds? Insofar as we are Christians we shall stress both. The popular pose of those who claim that words are not needed, because deeds are everything, have missed the important point that the best deeds *are* words. Frequently, the words that we are able to say to a distraught or confused person help that person most. What you remember most gratefully may be something that someone *said* to you long ago. It is not enough to give a cup of cold water; it is necessary also to tell *why*.

Much of the answer to polarization is to be found in a new conception of ecumenicity. What is required in this conception is not church union, which may or may not develop, but a new understanding of the meaning of "and." The combination we seek is that which unites the different aspects of an individual's faith. Important as unity in the churches may be, the unity of individual lives is still more important, because it is prior. We seek a unity both of tense and of mood.

It is necessary to see clearly that it is a mistake to place exclusive trust in the experience of the present, just as it is a mistake to trust only the past. The person who is concerned only with what is gone is hardly alive, while the person who is concerned with only the present has a life empty of content. Since the facts that we know by memory, or by the reports of those whom we have reason to trust, vastly outnumber those that we know by immediate experience, unwillingness to learn from earlier experience simply means intellectual and spiritual impoverishment. If we reject ideas from an earlier century *because* they are earlier, we are logically driven to reject those of the past year, the past day, and even the past hour. This is where the doctrine of bare contemporaneity would lead, if those who profess it were to be sincere, and should be honest enough to accept the logical implications of their basic proposition. They would be as shallow as the Athenians and foreigners who, at the time of the Apostle Paul's visit to Athens, "spent their time in nothing except telling or hearing something new" (Acts 17:21).

The same is true of the need for both reason and passion. The man of reason, devoid of passion, becomes bloodless, while the man of passion, devoid of reason, has no way of resisting the appeal of any dogma or even of superstition. The lessons of history are replete with this double truth. The only person who is able to operate effectively in our complex age is one who recognizes that there is no incompatibility between the warm heart and the clear head. The new Christian man, who can give leadership for the new day, is the one who, without even a hint of contradiction, can enjoy studying the works of Aristotle and, on the same day, appreciate singing "Jesus, Lover of My Soul." The worst mark of confusion is the prejudice that a man cannot do both. Those who demonstrate, without apology or undue self-consciousness, that they *can* do both, will be respected and followed. They will be able to make something of the impact upon our time that William Temple made upon his, when his characteristic titles were *Christus Veritas* and *Mens Creatrix.*

We face at this point a paradox in moral philosophy which demands careful attention if confusion is to be avoided. It is true that happiness also comes from within; it comes from focusing attention upon ourselves. In one sense our inner life is our hope, but in another sense our inner life is our terrible danger. The problem is resolved if we realize that the beneficent inner secret is that by which we learn to direct all our major attention and interest to something outside ourselves. Only the unified life brings true well-being, but the unity must be *directional* rather than substantive.

Each one of us is the scene of turmoil, with all kinds of competing motives, ambitions, emotions and desires. Many of our desires are in direct conflict with one another and thus every person is, at some time, a scene of civil war. There is a sense in which each individual is the complex monster of which Plato wrote in *The Republic.*

Whatever else about us is true, we may be sure that we cannot unify our divided and distracted lives from the *inside.* There is little point in the advice that we should follow our natural desires because these desires are so numerous and because, furthermore, many of them are mutually incompatible. There is a natural desire to be boastful and there is also a natural desire to have the approbation of our fellows, but it is very hard to satisfy both of these desires at once, since they cancel one another. As long as we try to unify our lives from within we fail, for again we reintroduce the disease into the supposed cure.

The only way in which a person may achieve relative unity of life is by dedication to something outside himself, to which he gives such loyal devotion that the self is forgotten in the process. The competing parts of our lives, which cannot unite of themselves, are then united because of a unity of direction, when all parts point one way. *The ancient truth is that the health of the self comes, not by concentrating on self, but by such dedication to something outside the self, that self is thereby forgotten.*

The Christian intellectual provides our best hope because he has access to both the reasons of the heart and the reasons of the head, and if he is worthy of his vocation he knows how to combine them. He can hold in one context both intellectual integrity and depth of spiritual experience, with no sense of incompatibility. In short, he can both pray and think! He will be keenly aware of the appeals of both agnosticism and dogmatism, but he will resist both, because both represent escape from the struggle for an intelligent faith. What we need is thoughtful people who belong to the fellowship of perplexity, yet have discovered points of clarity in the midst of the confusion. This is the strategy of Basic Christianity. We do not have certainty in the absolute sense Descartes sought, but we have a commitment which provides a starting point for all else. It is a mark of maturity to believe fewer doctrines, but to believe them with greater intensity.

In presenting Basic Christianity to seekers, it is particularly important to avoid the use of labels and artificial classifications. It is pointless to try to pigeonhole a man as a "liberal" or an "evangelical," for every sound Christian is both of these. He is an evangelical because he has settled one question: he is Christ-centered. But he is also a liberal because he is willing to learn from any source and to face new truth whenever and wherever it is revealed. How inept it is to suppose that a man is either a philosopher or one who accepts revelation, is made obvious when we consider the life and thought of William Temple of Canterbury. Temple was a big enough man to have more than one side to his life, and he combined them with éclat.

For the most part theological labels serve no useful purpose, because they tend to classify what cannot be classified without distortion. Labels, instead of encouraging thought, have the effect of diminishing it in that once a man's classification is known, there seems to be no need of further inquiry. Thus, when we call a man a conservative theologian, we feel that we can safely limit his influence to his particular party. Conservatism is not, however, the mark of a party, but something essential to the life of every thoughtful person. All intelligent people are conservatives, because they seek to conserve the accumulated wisdom of mankind. They are keenly aware of the fact that we are not rich enough in human resources to waste anything of tested value. But in the same way, every Christian theologian is radical in that he wants to go to the root of the matter. He is not willing to settle for mere priestcraft or ceremonial, and like Socrates he is willing to follow the evidence wherever it may lead. Only by a combination of conservatism and radicalism is progress possible. The people who are willing to end discussion by employing the old labels merely demonstrate that they have not caught up with the modern world.

The fallacy of easy classification is that of supposing that tendencies represent separate men, when in fact they usually represent competing elements within the lives of individual men. Almost every thinking person has a more or less continuous dialogue within his own consciousness. Though it is a mistake to settle for party tags, it is not a mistake to speak of competing tendencies. When we learn that Barth refuses to be considered a Barthian, we begin to understand that no great thinker is ever satisfied to be restricted to one classification. Such an example makes it necessary to point out that when we use terms ending in "ism," as is sometimes necessary, we are speaking more of tendencies than of groups of men.

In spite of all the variations of Christian belief, there has normally been, and there is now, a central stream of thought. What we denote as Basic Christianity is that which exists at the center of the Christian spectrum. Far from being sectarian, it is represented in nearly all denominations. This central stream is both rational and evangelical. The essential feature is commitment to Jesus Christ, who told His followers to love God with all their minds (Mark 12:30).

While there are many current evidences of decay, there is also a saving remnant, especially among those of the silent center. In spite of the much-publicized erosion of faith, large segments of our people accept Christ as the surest reality of their lives; they truly love God, and they engage in service to their fellow men which is motivated by this love. The strange fact, however, is that the vast majority of contemporary Christians have no adequate voice, because they have so few spokesmen to whom the intellectual world is willing to listen. The tendency is to give major attention, and the headlines, to faddists. We must develop spokesmen who are able to articulate the faith of the great body of Christians who, though they seldom speak up, are tremendously important.

The two great words of Christian history are *evangelical* and *catholic*. Both are so precious that it is a serious mistake to use them merely to refer to parties or denominations. Neither term should ever be permitted to become the monopoly or private possession of a single group, since each is too big for that! The reason why every genuine Christian is catholic is that Christ's call is universal. We are called to be the salt, not merely of a little group, but of the whole earth. In the same way every genuine Christian is evangelical, because a Christian is one who answers affirmatively the call, "Come to me" (Matthew 11:28).

Selections in Chapter Three are taken from:
The New Man for Our Time
The Common Ventures of Life
The Life We Prize
A Place to Stand

Chapter Four

THE USE OF
CHRISTIAN CLASSICS

*E*lton Trueblood's love of the Christian classics has been an important part of his life ever since he studied under Willard L. Sperry at Harvard. It was Sperry who first introduced the young Trueblood to the spiritual resources found within the pages of the great literary masterpieces, all of which have withstood the judgment of time. One of the most discouraging aspects of our contemporary life is found in our temporal snobbishness. We tend to suppose that new is better than old, but this is not necessarily true. In the words which follow, Elton Trueblood helps his readers to appreciate the value of the Christian classics, and points us on the upward way toward spiritual growth.

J.R.N.

The Church, if it is to affect the world, must become a center from which new spiritual power emanates. While the Church must be secular in the sense that it operates in the world, if it is only secular it will not have the desired effect upon the secular order which it is called upon to penetrate. With no diminution of concern for people, we can and must give new attention to the production of a trustworthy religious experience. In this understanding the devotional classics constitute a valuable resource.

One of the most remarkable features of the genuine classics of the inner life is their mutual corroboration. The religious experience of one man in one century may be suspected of having only subjective reference, but when the experiences are repeated in widely different cultures and epochs, we begin to have the only evidence of objectivity that men are never able to achieve. Just as agreement in experience is the only reason for asserting objectivity in science, so it is the only reason for asserting it in religion. In the effort to know what is true, the most important fellowship is the fellowship of verification, in which the experience of one man supports the credibility of the experience of another. In the words of William James, "There is a certain composite photograph of saintliness." Dean Inge gave expression to the entire logical structure of the experiential argument. "On all questions about religion," he said, "there is the most distressing divergency. But the saints do not contradict one another. They claim to have had glimpses of a land that is very far off, and they prove that they have been there by bringing back perfectly consistent and harmonious reports of it." Furthermore, said Inge, "We need not trouble outselves to ask, and we could seldom guess without asking, whether a paragraph describing the highest spiritual experiences was written in the Middle Ages or in modern times, in the north or south of Europe, by a Catholic or by a Protestant."

One of the most evident weaknesses of the contemporary church appears here. Even in an otherwise strong local church , it is not uncommon to find that most of the members, while they have undertaken some study of the Bible, particularly in Sunday School, are totally ignorant of the great chain of devotional literature extending from Augustine to Thomas Kelly and beyond. What is most surprising, in this connection, is the failure on the part of pastors to introduce those under their care to the acknowledged masters of the inner life. Though we might reasonably expect that almost every pastor would conduct classes pointed in this direction, only a tiny minority actually do so. The average pastor is a dedicated man eager to build up the spiritual life of the members and, through them, to affect the events of the world, but he normally omits one of the best ways of achieving this purpose. Pastors prepare sermons and visit families, but many seem to forget that in the New Testament the work of a pastor is linked to that of a teacher (Eph. 4:11). There is normally no lack of emphasis upon social issues, and this is good, but the odd outcome is that pastors seem to teach least in the very area in which they might be expected to have the greatest competence.

Because of the remarkable unanimity of judgment, the problem of selection among the classics is not a serious one. We have a manageable number of books on the cultivation of the interior life which have met the test of changing times and are therefore not on trial. Among these are the following:

The Confessions of St. Augustine.
The Imitation of Christ by Thomas á Kempis and others.
The Private Devotions of Lancelot Andrewes.
The Devotions of John Donne.
The Pensées of Blaise Pascal.
The Journal of John Woolman.
A Serious Call to a Devout and Holy Life by William Law.
A Testament of Devotion by Thomas Kelly.

These eight books are by no means all that serious seekers ought to study, but they are sufficient, when perused consecutively and prayerfully, to make a difference in almost any individual life. Though they can be studied profitably by lone individuals, they make more impact when studied with a group, because each student contributes to the others and thereby the experience is made richer.

It is a serious mistake to suppose that the only authors who are helpful in the development of a deeper religious experience are those normally classified as religious writers. As a matter of fact, some of the most helpful are those who are known almost solely as secular authors. An excellent example of such a group is Dr. Samuel Johnson (1709-1794). Part of the strength of such a guide, so far as modern man is concerned, resides precisely in the fact that, though he was thoroughly and unashamedly devout, Johnson was not professionally religious. The famous lexicographer was rough or even uncouth in his manners, and he was completely intolerant of cant or pretense, but his example of personal piety is all the more valuable in consequence. He helps us partly because he had, himself, been helped by other giants, chiefly Jeremy Taylor and William Law. He liked to remember, he said, the precept of Taylor, "Never lie in your prayers; never confess more than you really believe; never promise more than you mean to perform." William Law was, Johnson said, "more than a match" for him.

For those who are denied access to complete books, there is the possibility of concentrating upon selections. Further depth of understanding may come from the reading of the books of contemporary authors who have made it their task to interpret the works of the classic devotional writers. Among these, one of the most helpful is Rufus M. Jones, who, at the height of his powers, wrote books with such titles as *Spiritual Energies in Daily Life, The World Within,* and *The Testimony of the Soul.* In this last-mentioned volume, Dr. Jones, as early as 1936, undertook to write a chapter on the very topic that is concerning so many of us in the contemporary scene, "The Inner Life and the Social Order." Douglas V. Steere, Rufus Jones' immediate successor in the philosophy chair at Haverford College, has likewise contributed volumes of interpretation and analysis, introducing many readers to rich veins of which they would otherwise have been largely ignorant. Characteristic titles of Dr. Steere are *On Beginning from Within* and *Doors into Life*. The latter volume introduces the reader to five classics, *The Imitation of Christ, Introduction to the Devout Life* by Francis de Sales, John Woolman's *Journal*, Soren Kierkegaard's *Purity of Heart*, and the *Selected Letters* of Friedrich von Hugel.

Another important contemporary interpreter of classic spiritual experience is John Baillie, particularly in *A Dairy of Private Prayer* and *Christian Devotion*, the latter published posthumously by the efforts of his widow. In the United States one of the best of living interpreters is Howard Thurman, author of *The Inward Journey* and *Disciplines of the Spirit*. Dr. Thurman has profited greatly by his careful study of the Negro spirituals. An interpreter who is sorely missed is the late Thomas Kepler of Oberlin who, in spite of severe physical stress near the end of his life, found strength to bring out reprints of the books mentioned for the use of the general public.

Nearly all the classics of devotion have in common the conviction of the possibility and, indeed, actuality of the divine-human encounter. Impressed as the spiritual giants may be with the natural order, they are seldom willing to settle for this as the only or the sufficient revelation of the Divine Mind. Though most would agree with Wordsworth in his sense of reverence in the midst of natural beauty, they do not stop there. William Temple was representing faithfully the major tradition when, after speaking of God's revelation as an indirect one through the natural order, he went on to affirm the possibility and actuality of direct communication between God and the finite human soul. "It would be strange," Temple wrote, "if He acted only in the inorganic and non-spiritual, and dealt with spirits akin to Himself only by the indirect testimony of the rest of His creation."

In one excellent prayer group made up of men, the attenders soon began to find help from the Christian classics and were genuinely surprised by the freshness of the older insights. They wondered why they had to wait for full maturity, to learn even of the existence of some books of exciting worth. One such book which they came to appreciate was *A Serious Call to a Devout and Holy Life* by William Law, an eighteenth-century writer who influenced many in his day, including Dr. Samuel Johnson and John Wesley.

Much as the busy men in the prayer group were helped by the old book by William Law, all agreed that Law was terribly wordy and that many passages were redundant. As a practical consequence the men decided, with the help of their pastor who was also a member of the group, to try to reduce the book to a form in which it would be more profitable to contemporary readers. They worked on the project for about a hear and found that they loved it so much that they would try for publication. Now the reduced and substantially improved volume has been published by the Westminster Press and is available to all. This experience tells many lessons at once, including the lesson that people get more out of anything if they take an active part in it.

Not all religious experience is the same, but there are characteristic features which appear with astonishing regularity and which are not especially difficult to describe. Normally, it is not some experience wholly separated from other experiences, but a particular way in which all reality is apprehended. It comes about most naturally in the mood of prayer or worship, though it is by no means limited to stated times for these, either individually or collectively. Ordinarily religious experience has nothing to do with visions, ecstasies, raptures or other phenomena which are usually considered abnormal. It is true that some mystics have experienced these exalted states of consciousness or unconsciousness, but they are no part of *normative* religious experience. On the contrary, such experience is as unspectacular as breathing or sleeping. For most men and women, religious experience has been a calm assurance of the reality of a relationship which gives meaning to existence.

The author of the *Imitation of Christ* provides us with one of the most extensive examples of such personal testimony found in all literature. The book is a revelation, not only because of what one modest man experienced five hundred years ago, but also because of the way in which it has elicited a response from so many others in so many generations and cultures.

Always the emphasis of the *Imitation* is on firsthand experience, which is declared to be superior to all indirect ways of knowing God. "Let not Moses nor any other of the prophets speak to me, but rather Thou, Lord, that art the inward inspirer and giver of light to all prophets; for Thou only, without them, mayst fully inform me and instruct me; they, without Thee, may little profit me." Always the Fountain is more to be valued than anything which flows from the Fountain. The man who has known God face to face values the Giver more than the gift. The result of such immediate contact is a wonderful sense of joy. At no point is this said more vividly than in the following sentences:

> Ah, my Lord God, most faithful lover, when thou comest into my heart, all that is within me doth joy! Thou art my glory and the joy of my heart, my hope and my whole refuge in all my troubles.

The more we know of the background out of which such a testimony comes the harder it is to ridicule it. "No other book, except the Bible," says Rufus M. Jones, "Has been a more permanent source of joy and comfort and hope." Here is a witness which it is very hard to neglect or to disdain, because it is so obviously modest and sane.

Another excellent example of the written testimony is the

record of Blaise Pascal, memorializing his keen sense of God's presence which came to him on November 23, 1654. Pascal sewed the report in his coat, where it was found by his servant after his death. He valued the memory of the experience so highly that it affected the remainder of his days.

In trying to state faithfully what occurred, this brilliant man wrote what was essentially a string of interjections. The word "fire" was the most emphasized of all, probably in an effort to say that what was perceived had about it the same indubitable quality that we find in the flame which warms, lights, and even burns.

The importance of this witness is increased in our estimation as we remind ourselves of the kind of man Pascal was. He was one of the world's really great mathematicians, he was an excellent scientist, and he was a transparently good man. But, in spite of his learning, he was, in effect, repeating the famous judgment of the *Imitation of Christ*, "I had rather feel compunction than be able to give the most accurate definition of it." He valued his acquaintance with God far more than his knowledge about God.

A second source of reports is the specifically religious autobiography, particularly the journal of the inner life. Such an account is fuller than that of the separated report, often showing how an entire life has been guided by God's love. During the first hundred years of the Quaker Movement it was practically standard for leading Quakers to write journals, and all of them were written with the same purpose in mind. The beginning of the *Journal of George Fox* makes this purpose wholly clear. "That all may know the dealings of the Lord with me, and the various exercises, trials and troubles through which He led me in order to prepare and fit me for the work unto which He had appointed me, and may thereby be drawn to admire and glorify his infinite wisdom and goodness, I think fit briefly to mention how it was with me in my youth, and how the work of the Lord was begun and gradually carried on in me, even from my childhood." It must be understood that the best of this literature of witness has not come from those who can, in any sense, be called professionals, but often from modest people who have no reason to tell what their experience of God is except the natural desire to share with others what is precious. Our time has been marked by a renewal of interest in the devotional classics, a number of scholars giving us interpretations and fresh editions.

By the time of my arrival at Harvard, Willard L. Sperry was dean of the Divinity School and also dean of the Chapel. From the beginning he took a close personal interest in me and finally became my tutor, criticizing my papers in a regular and meticulous fashion. Later it pleased me greatly when Dean Sperry asked me to be acting dean of the Chapel at Harvard for the summer of 1935 and acting professor of the Philosophy of Religion in the autumn of 1944. His greatest academic assistance, so far as I was concerned, arose from our mutual examination of the Christian classics of devotion and the long poems of William Wordsworth. In frequent private meetings Dean Sperry urged me to soak myself in the great models, apart from which advice I might not have begun my contact with the works of Dr. Samuel Johnson. Thus I became involved in what Whitehead called "the habitual vision of greatness." Others to whom Dean Sperry introduced me as masters of style were William Hazlitt and Olive Schreiner.

Guilford College, when we arrived in September 1927, was in the country, six miles out the Friendly Road from Greensboro. Today the population has grown so much that the Guilford campus is actually in the city. Having been founded by North Carolina Quakers in 1837, the college was a well-respected institution with about four hundred students equally divided between women and men. We were assigned the use of a small house on the wooded campus close enough to the dormitories to bring us into contact with the students at all times. As dean of men I had an office in one of the dormitories and found it possible to know by name nearly all of the men as well as some of the women. Martin, who was two years old, soon learned to wander about the campus and became a welcome visitor in student rooms.

I tried to combine lectures and seminars, the latter being devoted to the study of major philosophical works. Because reprints were rather inexpensive, it was reasonable to expect even the students who were on low budgets to purchase the classics, which they might keep all of their lives as cherished possessions. One enterprise which provided me much satisfaction was my first course in Christian Classics, modeled to some extent on that taught by Dean Sperry at Harvard. I soon found that is was comparatively easy to interest students in the works of Augustine, à Kempis, and Pascal because the thoughts of these men are not limited to their time. My own mind grew as I attempted my first teaching, some of the books which I analyzed being then read by me for the first time.

The metaphor of the journey has been particularly appealing, especially to committed Christians who are aware that in the earliest days the followers of Christ were known as Those of the Way. That is why John Baillie entitled his brilliant introduction to Christianity *Invitation to Pilgrimage*. All literate people owe a debt in this connection to John Bunyan, his *Pilgrim's Progress* having become long ago an essential feature of our intellectual and spiritual climate. Apart from Bunyan, Lord Tweedsmuir would not have called his own memoirs *Pilgrim's Way*. What is most attractive about the entire conception of life as a journey is the widespread realization that no man walks alone. Others walk with us now, encountering some of the same problems as they proceed, and many others have trod the same general path in earlier centuries. My four shelves of devotional classics are, I recognize, filled with what are essentially guidebooks. They tell of the pitfalls on the road, and they indicate where the rewarding views are. The farther I proceed, the more I am indebted to those who have left, for me and for others, what Professor Baillie termed "fingerposts," pointing the way.

Selections in Chapter Four are taken from:
The New Man for Our Time
The Yoke of Christ
Philosophy of Religion
While It Is Day

Chapter Five

THE
REDEMPTIVE FELLOWSHIP

T he redemptive fellowship has been a major concern of Elton Trueblood throughout his long and active ministry. Following the pattern of the Early Church, Dr. Trueblood challenges his readers to discover the valuable spiritual possibilities that the small Christian group can offer. Disciplined in its inner life of devotion, active in its outer life of ministry, and committed to a life of study, the redemptive fellowship offers the world islands of hope amidst a sea of despair. In this chapter the idea is given practical form, and offers the reader an alternative to the secularism which is infecting our age.

J.R.N.

Somewhere in the world there should be a society consciously and deliberately devoted to the task of seeing how love can be made real and demonstrating love in practice. Unfortunately, there is really only one candidate for this task. If God, as we believe, is truly revealed in the life of Christ, the most important thing to Him is the creation of centers of loving fellowship, which in turn infect the world. Whether the world can be redeemed in this way we do not know, but it is at least clear that there is no other way.

As I came into middle age, two separate dangers were simultaneously impressed upon my mind. I saw, at the same time, both the futility of empty freedom and the fruitlessness of single effort. Affirmatively stated, the latter led to the idea of the small fellowship, while the former led to the idea of voluntary discipline; in conjunction they led to the recognition that hope lies in the creation of an order. Now, for a quarter of a century, much of my thought and energy have been employed in both the dream and its embodiment in one particular order, the Order of the Yoke.

The conviction that in the promotion of the Christian Cause a new approach is needed, was deeply impressed upon me in my final years as chaplain of Stanford University. I began to see where the power is, and where it is not. I observed among our soldier students the obvious strength of the Orthodox Jews with whom I met in the vestry of Memorial Church on Friday evenings. Their cohesiveness and their personal discipline were two sides of the same pattern of living. In contrast to the attendance at a conventional student gathering, which was always unpredictable, the attendance of Orthodox Jews on Friday nights sometimes amounted to 100 percent of those involved. They were faithful and they were participants largely because they had a rule by which they undertook to live. Suddenly I saw that those young men, though they were not Christians, exhibited some of the characteristics of the Christian orders about which I read with interest and admiration.

The spiritual growth at Stanford in 1945 was the consequence of small committed and disciplined groups. Beginning with one group which met in the chapel for prayer every noon, the movement grew until there were such groups in every living unit throughout the entire campus. The Chapel Cabinet was remodeled into a group which included prayer as well as discussion and action, and in which each member began to accept a serious discipline of the interior life. Without conscious intention, something of the character of an order was actually emerging.

During those days I thought a great deal of what orders had meant in the history of the Christian faith, especially after I read the life of St. Francis by G. K. Chesterton. Much as I admired the work of the First Order and the Second Order of St. Francis, I admired the Third Order most because it was envisioned as a way of meeting the needs of those who were involved in common life. At Stanford the idea was so infectious that some of the members of the Chapel Cabinet began calling themselves "tertiaries." We were convinced that far from needing any new denominations, we may actually be entering the post-denominational age. We knew that whereas denominations have existed for only about four hundred years, orders have existed far longer. The effectiveness of the Benedictine Order, especially in the penetration of pagan England, is impressive to anyone who knows the story. Perhaps, we said, we require contemporary orders, developed in our own century; we need not, we said, depend wholly upon former patterns because new ones can emerge now.

When we referred to an order, we meant something radically different from a denomination; we envisioned a horizontal fellowship, cutting across existing religious lines. The new grouping, we thought, would not supplant the existing churches nor work against them, but would rather work *within* them for the purpose of renewal. We saw that our deepest fellowships, far from being limited to our own denominations, tend to transcend them, some of our best friendships being with those who are members of bodies other than our own. That indeed is part of what is meant in calling ours a post-denominational age, though emphatically it need not be a post-Christian age. The members of the emerging order, we saw, are marked both by the intensity of their fellowship and by their spiritual self-discipline. Instead of being permissive with themselves, they are tough, and in spite of their failures, they have a rule by which they seek to live. Such a rule naturally is very different from that of any medieval order in that it is one appropriate to life in the modern world. The new rule which must be developed, far from being geared to life in a monastery, is one made by and for men and women who, because they have children to rear, taxes to pay, and work to do, cannot be cloistered.

Two important steps, so far as my own thinking was concerned, came in August 1948 and in May 1949. The former came in my visit to Iona, when I participated for the first time in the Iona Fellowship. I saw that under the inspiring leadership of George MacLeod, a new order had actually arisen, with the work of St. Columba as its model. At Iona I saw a developed pattern which included interior discipline, ministry, evangelism, and social action. The discipline of beginning each day with prayer, seeking to go through the day in prospect, and asking God's guidance upon each detail, appealed to me so mightily that I have sought ever since, not only to practice it myself, but also to lead others into it. The rhythm of withdrawal and encounter, basic to the Iona pattern of Christian vocation, is obviously sound. On Sunday, when I was present, the sermon delivered in the restored Cathedral of the Isles was entitled "The Mountain and the Plain," a message based upon Mark 9:2-29. The fact that Christ withdrew to the mountain retreat even while the people needed Him, and later returned to them in human service, was to me a fresh insight. I saw that such a rhythm must be an essential element of any new order worth developing in our generation.

The crucial experience came in May 1949, nine months after the first visit to Iona. Having promised to preach on Sunday at the First Baptist Church of Cleveland, I traveled by Pullman train from Dayton so as to have a good night's rest and if possible to be alert on Sunday morning. After completing my sleep and a quiet breakfast in the Terminal Building, I boarded the Rapid Transit for Cleveland Heights. Already, under the influence of Frank Laubach, I had begun the practice of reading every morning from the New Testament, whatever my location might be. Instead of skipping about in the Scriptures, I had adopted the discipline of going straight through a book, reading slowly about eleven verses a day if the topic admitted such a division, and noting, in the margin, the place and date of reading. This system of dating has come to be personally valuable in that my New Testament has in one sense become also my diary. Many different copies of the New Testament have now been dated in this fashion, and these become reminders of high moments in a quarter century.

My reading that morning on the Rapid Transit was Matthew 11:25-30. Though I had of course read the passage on many former occasions, it struck me then with unique force. It was almost as though I had never before read the words "Take my yoke upon you." Suddenly, I saw that this is Christ's clearest call to commitment. I realized that the yoke metaphor involves what we most require if the vitality of the Christian faith is to be recovered. Being yoked with Christ may mean a great deal more, but at least it means being a participant rather than a spectator; it also means accepting a discipline which leads paradoxically to a new kind of freedom; it leads finally to fellowship because the yokes which we know best cannot be worn alone. Within a minute or so, as an entire complex of thinking came together, I had a different sermon. In my briefcase was a sermon which I had prepared, but I have no idea what its subject was, for it was entirely supplanted by a new and exciting vision. The words which came to me on the train that morning I preached within the hour, recognizing that I was participating in a new development. Later, when I wrote as faithfully as I could what I had said that morning, it became the first chapter of the book *The Yoke of Christ.*

Suddenly, in 1949, we had a name for our hitherto nameless fellowship which was beginning to be a conscious one. We saw that the term "Yokefellow," which is employed in the New Testament (Philippians 4:3) as a synonym for a practicing Christian, derives its entire significance from the yoke passage on which I had felt led to speak at the First Baptist Church of Cleveland. The advantages of the term "Yokefellow" are obvious in that it is a Biblical term and is also free from the ambiguity of the word "cell." Furthermore, it provides a suitable nomenclature for the growing number of men and women who are unwilling to be known as either laymen or clergymen. Thus it appeared to be a genuine third way, and some grasped it eagerly.

It is good to remember that the revolutionary fellowship, of which we read in the New Testament, was a result of careful thought and much disciplined dreaming. In our sense the entire burst of new life was undoubtedly the work of God, a gift of divine grace, like the spirit which bloweth where it listeth; but in another sense the work and thought of dedicated men was required. Not only are the major portions of the Gospels devoted to the careful elaboration of this intensive fellowship but, likewise, the Epistles of St. Paul involve many contributions to the general problem. The Pauline Epistles are given over, in considerable measure, to creative thought about what the nature of a redeeming fellowship might be. In letter after letter the same criteria appear. The fellowship must be marked by mutual affection of the members, by a sense of real equality in spite of difference of function, by inner peace in the face of the world's turmoil and by an almost boisterous joy. The members are to be filled, not with the intoxication of wine, but with that of the Spirit. Such people could hardly avoid, as the sequence in the fifth chapter of Ephesians suggests, breaking out in psalms and hymns. In the early Christian community the people sang, not from convention, but from a joy which overflowed. Life for these people was no longer a problem to solve but a glory to discern.

We are so hardened to the story that it is easy for us to forget how explosive and truly revolutionary the Christian faith was in the ancient Mediterranean world. The Church at first had no buildings, no separated clergy, no set ritual, no bishops, no pope, yet it succeeded in turning life upside down for millions of unknown men and women, giving them a new sense of life's meaning and superb courage in the face of persecution or sorrow. It is our tragedy that we are living in a day when much of this primal force is spent. Our temper is so different that we hardly understand what the New Testament writers are saying. Once a church was a brave and revolutionary fellowship, changing the course of history by the introduction of discordant ideas; today it is a place where people go and sit on comfortable benches, waiting patiently until time to go home to their Sunday dinners.

The idea of a redemptive fellowship, so amazingly central to Christianity, involves an entire philosophy of civilization. How is civilization changed? It is changed, early Christianity answers, by the creation of fellowships which eventually become infectious in the entire cultural other. We are surprised to see how little the early Christians dealt with current political and economic problems, if we may judge by the extant literature of the period. They did not even attack slavery, iniquitous as it must have been. They just went on building the kind of fellowship that was bound, eventually, to destroy slavery. All this seems alien to our modern mentality, but it may involve divine wisdom. In any case, we should not be too proud to try, for we are not doing so well on our present line of endeavor. It helps our modesty to realize that these ancient men were accused of turning the world upside down, whereas no one would accuse us of anything similar. Instead of turning the world upside down, we feel helpless as we watch the rising spiral of inflationary prices, observe with some foreboding the actions of little men in Washington and go to the races.

The sense of membership in a redemptive society would dignify individual lives in that it would give meaning to history, along with a sense of human solidarity, since membership involves men in a longitudinal, as well as latitudinal, fellowship. There has been an enduring and continuous community, beginning with a suppressed people who were preserved through all kinds of danger for the sake of a divine purpose which was destined to include all humanity. The heroes and prophets of this tradition may be spiritual ancestors of us all regardless of our biological inheritance. The story is a very old story, with a historical dialectic of its own. Glorious as Israel was, it required both transcendence and fulfillment in the formation of another community, equally dedicated, but by no means limited to one nation or race, and thus universal. Early Christians were thrilled as they thought of themselves as part of this emerging divine purpose. They had a link with eternity because in their fellowship they were partners in the creative love that made the world.

It is perfectly clear that the same method could be effective again, if we could have the simplicity to try it. Men who are partners in the redemptive task of God Himself have all the dignity of personal life that is required to lift them out of mediocrity, but their glorification does not come at the expense of others or by means of antagonism. It was a cardinal point in the redemptive fellowships which changed the ancient world that all human barriers must be transcended. There is no longer Jew or Gentile, no longer bond or free. The work is grounded in history, quite as truly as the work of the convinced Nazi or the convinced Communist, but it involves no struggle against other races or other classes. It takes man as man, wherever he may be, and binds him into a loving fellowship which acknowledges Jesus Christ as the Lord of Life and which believes that humble men and women may be partners of the divine will. Their creed is summarized by the conviction that "In all things, God works for good *with* them who love him."

The saving faith we need will not come of itself but must be consciously fostered and spread. It was in this kind of work that Augustine and his associates were so successful in the dark times following the decline of Roman culture. They made a church adequate to meet the needs of the time, something that could survive even when the empire went to pieces. The close parallel already suggested makes it reasonable to suppose, in advance of specific arguments, that our central need is for a contemporary redemptive society which will do for us what the redemptive society envisaged by Augustine did for his generation and for succeeding generations. Christianity won in the Roman Empire, not chiefly as a belief, though it was a belief, but more as a self-conscious fellowship, and there is nothing in subsequent history to make us suppose that the faith adequate for our day will win in any other way.

What is required to save us from the destruction of which world wars constitute a foretaste is a new spirit. We need this far more desperately than we need any new machine or anything else. We are fairly clear concerning the nature of this new spirit, since it has been tested repeatedly in the religious tradition out of which our highest moral standards have come, even though it is now so largely ignored. We must spread this spirit by the written and spoken word, as many are already doing, though nowhere is sufficient force. But we must go beyond this to the formation of cells, made up of men and women who are as single-minded in their devotion to the redemptive task as the early Nazi party members were to the task of National Socialism.

The kind of organized movement that the need of the hour suggests does not at present exist. Certainly the existent church cannot function in this way because *Christianity has long ceased to be scrupulous in membership.* Some may be members because they are greatly concerned over the redemption of our civilization, but they are surrounded by millions who are members because they were born that way or because membership helps their social standing. Since the devoted and effective group cannot be *found,* it must be *made.*

The present is the time for some creative and urgent dreaming about the nature of the redemptive society that is so clearly necessary. This society may be as different from the conventional church of today as an airplane is different from a buggy. But just as a buggy and an airplane have the same fundamental purpose, namely, transportation, so the church of today and the religious society of tomorrow may have the same redemptive purpose, though new problems require new vision.

Here lies a path of redemption for which many in the modern world are waiting, even though they do not realize what it is they seek. There is a vast amount of loneliness, and a consequent desire to belong to something. This is shown by the success of the new cults and by the emergence of groups in which fellowship is genuine, even though, as judged by conventional standards, hardly respectable. For example, the organization called Alcoholics Anonymous appears to have an enormous influence in the lives of its members. Its paradoxical entrance qualifications sound peculiarly Christian, in that each man must admit that he is too weak to help himself and that each undertakes to help another.

Real fellowship is so rare and so precious that it is like dynamite in any human situation. Any group that will find a way to the actual sharing of human lives will make a difference either for good or ill in the modern world or in any world. But fellowship is always more likely to be genuine if men are united *for* something. The problem of purpose, however, really solves itself, so far as the present discussion is concerned. Those who see the danger in which our civilization lies and who have some intimation of the spiritual renewal without which our present order cannot possibly be saved have a ready-made purpose to draw them together. What we want is a group so devoted to this purpose and so tightly organized that it can work as effectively for redemptive ends in our time as the first Christians worked for redemptive ends in the first century of our era and as the Nazis have worked for divisive ends in the first century of their would-be era.

We now have a clue which may guide us in the recovery of a sense of meaning in our lives. We find this clue in the concept of faith through a special kind of fellowship. It is something which was once proposed, once tried and once found to succeed. That it succeeded so abundantly is our chief basis of hope, because there is reason to believe that *what has been can again be.* In our dire extremity, marked especially by a sense of futility, we are justified in turning with hope to the most striking example of spiritual revival which the history of the world can show.

In turning to this example we need to remind ourselves again that that with which we are dealing is sober history. The redemptive effect of the little Christian community on the ancient civilized world is no fairy story. It is not a fantastic tale produced by an imaginative writer; it is not a philosophy of civilization which some thinker constructed in the privacy of his study; *it occurred.* Conscious of a divine destiny and filled with love of the brethren, the little groups, once established at Philippi, Corinth and Ephesus, finally altered the structure and tone of ancient culture.

Here then is our clue. The method which succeeded before must be tried again and we must not be dismayed by its amazing simplicity. The best chance for the renewal of the human spirit in the twentieth century, as in the first, lies in the formation of genuinely redemptive societies in the midst of ordinary society. Such fellowships could provide a sense of meaning for the members within the societies and, at the same time, maintain an infectious influence on the entire culture outside. This is what occurred magnificently in the first century of our era and has occurred in lesser ways in other centuries, whenever really powerful forms of fellowship arose, as in the case of the early Franciscan soldiers of the seventeenth century. Our task now is to repeat the miracle of history. It seems unfortunate that so heavy a burden should rest on an instrument so fragile, but there is no other way. *That is the kind of world ours is.*

Unless it involves *fellowship* that is deep and inclusive, church membership is always nominal rather than real. Without genuine fellowship there is no *koinonia*. There are, indeed, times in our lives when we wish to enter a darkened church, pray and leave without speaking to another human being, but such religious experience is not satisfactory as a steady diet. The normal religious experience is that in which the society of worship becomes also a society of friends. We must be *disciples*, we must be *catholics*, but, above all, we must be *brethren*. Inner illumination alone, important as it is, may produce the self-centered and the bizarre, with no outside checks on either ideas or conduct. The sense of urgency alone may produce unbalanced fanaticism, but men and women who submit to the disciplines of fellowship, seeking group guidance in major decisions and recognizing the authority of group experience, are largely saved from these extravagances. The lesson of many religious societies is that, while individual mysticism may be dangerous, group mysticism tends to be wholly beneficient.

If Jesus is right, if the redemptive fellowship is really the salt of the earth, here is a place where each humble person can begin, no matter how frustrating the world complexity may seem. Here is truly a place to start on a job matched to our size. No one can stop us in our effort to form disciplined and loving fellowships, beginning in our homes. We have, in this undertaking, an effective antidote to discouragement in the realization that we are not working alone in our human power. The plan of world regeneration we are seeking to follow is not the result of human ingenuity but is part of the expressed purpose of the Son of God. Our planet may experience a real catastrophe and millions may die before their time, but it will still be God's world and His ultimate victory is assured. Even if another war comes, and civilization is more nearly destroyed than it now is, we, if we are still alive, can proceed with the Christian formula for world renewal.

We need not despise any effort, no matter how secular, which aims at world reconstruction, but we are very sure concerning what the primary and central need is. We need a new sense of life's meaning to end our mood of futility, and this comes only by a saving faith. The faith, in turn, is nurtured by a special kind of fellowship in which Christ himself is the central member. It is our holy privilege to help to nourish such fellowships. If enough persons do the same, we shall have a new world.

Usually, in our characteristic Christian gatherings, whether large or small, all of the talk flows one way, from the platform to the hall, but a contemporary small group breaks this pattern completely. Many of the changes in lives occur because the participants come to have a wholly new understanding of their responsibilities, when they realize that they are supposed to be the ones who pray, who advise one another, who admit their needs, and who plan together some modest steps in the advancement of Christ's Kingdom.

Often there is a good deal of prayer for specific individuals. Thus, in an effective prayer group made up of male college students, someone present will bring up the name of a person for whom he asks prayer, and all the young men respond by saying the person's name in unison. Then they pray silently for him and perhaps some will go on to pray audibly. Sometimes the problem of someone not present or even the problem of one of the attenders is presented in detail. All of this helps to avoid self-centeredness in the praying of the individuals who make up the group.

On the whole, experience shows that in such a group it is good to introduce, sooner or later, at least three elements, prayer, study, and discussion. If there is nothing but prayer the mood runs the risk of being in-grown; if there is nothing but study it tends to become academic; if there is nothing but discussion it may become superficial. But the combination of all three is remarkably fruitful.

As the growth of small fellowships continues, we may expect new and creative developments. One such development, which has come as a great surprise to many, is the establishment of a Yokefellow Group in a federal prison. A number of prisoners have built up, since they started in 1955, a really remarkable fellowship of prayer, of study, and of Christian witness. Each alone, as he faces the ridicule of the other prisoners, has a hard time in trying to maintain his conscious Christian discipleship, but the members find that the backing of the other committed ones is of immense help. In a way which those in civil life find difficult to understand, the fellowship of the committed group within prison walls is truly redemptive. Consequently they have much to teach us who are outside. The men have a common predicament, a common penitence, and a common faith which, in their meetings, they share with one another. That their lives are radically changed, both within the prison and after they are paroled, is not surprising. The fact that so much power can emerge in such an unlikely place should stimulate our minds to think of other ways in which the principles of redemptive fellowship can be applied. The probability is that we are still only at the beginning of what may be accomplished in this way: we have hardly scratched the surface. The meaning of "two or three together" is something which is bound to grow in our minds, as we seek humbly to be led along this fruitful path. The wonder is that God has shown us, right in the midst of our troubled time, something that brings freshness to the Christian movement. The power which has emerged in the fellowship of small groups is something which may rightly cause us to thank God and take courage.

The future of the Yoke we cannot know, but we are at least convinced that certain features are of enduring value. If they decline in one pattern, they will need to arise in some other. The essentials are *commitment, discipline, ministry,* and *fellowship.* Without the *commitment* nothing else of any importance will occur; unless there is *discipline,* life dissolves in permissiveness; the *ministry* is too important to be limited to a professional class; *fellowship* is essential because no person is strong enough to operate alone. The heart of the idea which has helped to give meaning to my own life for a quarter century is that, to be a Christian, *I must be yoked with others because I am yoked with Christ.*

Modest as our new order is, this one or something like it is what our time sorely needs, for it provides an alternative both to solitariness and the impersonalism of the crowd. I have been convinced that in the Christian Movement there will always be new and unexpected developments generation after generation. Just when the bones seem hopelessly dried, life arises. When I become discouraged, as I sometimes do, I remember the surprising creation of the Third Order of St. Francis seven hundred and fifty years ago. In like manner I think of the way in which the mood on both sides of the Atlantic was revolutionized by the Wesleys in the middle of the eighteenth century.

Each new development has been strictly unpredictable. Who could have predicted the work of Robert Raikes, in starting Sunday schools in 1780; or of George Williams, in dreaming up the Young Men's Christian Association in 1844; or of General William Booth, in establishing the Salvation Army in 1878? With such undoubted examples of inner renewal in mind, I expect others of equal significance in my lifetime, though I cannot possibly guess what their precise character will be.

The Yokefellow Movement is best understood as part of the Renewal Movement of the twentieth century. Far from operating alone, it is closely affiliated with numerous other new forms of Christian fellowship. Going beyond the development envisaged by Francis, these together constitute a kind of "Fourth Order." Transcending the distinction between Protestant and Catholic, and including both pastors and ordinary members, they establish centers, bearing various names, which are necessary for the continuing reformation within the churches.

Twenty-five years ago I wrote in my journal that we need a contemporary counterpart of the Salvation Army. What I then envisioned was a fellowship that would do for the average thoughtful person what the Salvation Army has done for the poor and the dispossessed. I saw that even the people who denounce the Church do not denounce the Salvation Army because its devotion is obviously genuine. The Army has provided countless modest persons with a faith, a discipline, and a means of witness. I hope to live long enough to rejoice in new developments as effective as the one which Booth created nearly a century ago. It will not surprise me if the last quarter of the century with which my life has so far been contemporary becomes one of the most productive of all history, so far as the Christian faith is concerned. One of the most encouraging ideas which has entered my mind is that we are *early Christians,* still alive while the faith is fluid and capable of assuming new forms. I think that this idea was originated by Professor Kenneth Scott Latourette, but the origin is not really important. The important fact is that it is true.

Selections in Chapter Five are taken from:
The Company of the Committed
While It Is Day
Alternative to Futility
The Predicament of Modern Man
The Yoke of Christ

Chapter
Six

THE
CHRISTIAN HOME

*N*ever before in the history of Western Civilization has the family been under such attack, and the sad reality that we must face is the fact that the attack is succeeding. In this chapter Elton Trueblood draws his readers back to the true meaning and purpose of the home, as understood from a Christian perspective. This unique understanding is a powerful antidote to the challenges which now threaten the Christian home, and if the suggestions offered are followed, the home can again become the redemptive element this society so desperately needs to help it survive.

J.R.N.

Of all human events, none more easily becomes an occasion for rejoicing than does marriage. Death is solemnizing, but marriage is both solemnizing and joyous at the same moment. Even the dullest person alive can hardly fail to have a sense of wonder as he sees a man and woman take their places before an altar and pledge their lifelong devotion to each other. Much of the art and much of the science of our world are efforts to find unity in diversity, the artist suffusing an entire scene with a single mood and the scientist finding a single law demonstrated in apparently diverse phenomena, but every marriage goes further. Marriage not only *discovers* unity; it undertakes to *create* unity, and to create in the most important areas of experience.

Two lives, belonging to different sexes, and often with widely different biological background, come together in the sight of God and before their friends to inaugurate something never seen in the world before—their particular combination of inheritance and their particular union of personalities. They join their destinies in such a manner that sorrow for one will be sorrow for the other and good fortune for one will be good fortune for the other. Moreover, both they and their friends are keenly aware that the normally expected result of their union will be the coming into the world of new persons, who, apart from this union, would never been granted the boon of existence.

It is this overpowering sense of *possibility* that makes even the most unostentatious wedding so moving an occasion. Those who join their destinies in marriage are, by their very togetherness, sharing in the entire creative process in a unique way. Marriage is a window through which the meaning of existence shines with unusual brilliance, and the window can never be so smudged that it wholly excludes that light.

We understand better the way in which marriage is fraught with tremendous possibility when we think of its range of failure and success as well as its potential pains and joys. It is perfectly clear, on the one hand, that the possibility of sorrow is greater in married life than in single life. The outcome may range from that of the death of one partner or the failure of affection which is worse than death, to the glory of continual growth in creative union. Each person who marries opens himself voluntarily to pain, because he puts himself in a position in which he can more easily be hurt. The person who has not made the wager of devotion cannot be hurt by the unfaithfulness of another as can the person who makes the leap of faith. Every avowed lover is terribly vulnerable, and marriage only accentuates the vulnerability as it accentuates the possible glory. The married woman, especially if she is carrying a child, has put herself in a position of grave economic inequality in case her husband should abandon her without support. Her life would have been far easier, in every way, had she never married. Those who never gamble cannot lose.

Sometimes married life, instead of bringing these sharp pains, brings something which may, in the end, be worse: the constant mutual nagging of persons whose lives are unsuited to one another or who are unwilling to undergo the disciplines of character which successful marriage requires. What Thoreau said about his neighbors with their lives of "quiet desperation" applies to many marriages which do not end in the public failure which we call divorce, but continue unhappily and ingloriously until one partner dies. The truth is that many are worse off in the married state than they would have been if they had remained single, for while the married life can be far happier than the single life, it can also be far more wretched. Those who wish to avoid all risk are advised to remain single.

There is a true sense in which every family is potentially a *holy family*. A mother, a father and little children conduct together an amazing experiment, often in marked contrast to the ways of the world for, in this tiny community, the harsh individualism of the ordinary struggle for existence is consciously and explicitly renounced. The rule is, "From each according to ability and to each according to need." The father, though he works very hard at exacting labor, often receives less from the family budget than does one of the tiny children, especially when the child is ill. The question of what each has contributed is an irrelevant question when the good things are divided. In war-torn Europe the mother who stands in line for food and who works long hours, often eats less than her caloric share, in order that the children may have more than their share. This is one of the chief reasons why the children of Germany appear in better health than observers expect to find. Their mothers do not.

The revival of the sense of the individual family as a holy experiment would do wonders in our present perplexed and perplexing culture. The great problems seem so nearly insoluble that the individual often feels helpless. We want to *lift*, but we cannot find a convenient or usable handle. Those in ordinary civil life feel helpless because the government does not do more, but those in government, even at the top, feel helpless too. Frequently their hands are tied by prior commitments and by pressures which they are unable to resist. Much of our economic activity is similarly baffling, for the system seems to be larger and toughter than the men who have made it. Steinbeck, in one of his novels, has expressed this sense of frustration by making one of his characters say, "The bank is something else than men. It happens that every man in a bank hates what the bank does, and yet the bank does it. The bank is something more than men, I tell you. It's the monster. Men made it, but they can't control it."

All who feel this sense of helplessness in the face of the magnitude of the modern world can derive hope from the possibilities of any modest family. Here *is* a handle by which we can life. A family is a unit of such manageable size that we can do in it what we cannot do elsewhere. Within the family there is not perfect harmony, but there is a constantly accepted ideal. In the individual home it is possible to establish our own standards, determine the nature of the major influences and make a separated area of cooperation in the midst of the world's competitive struggle. Each home, imperfect though it may be, is our closest approximation to the Kingdom of God. The ultimate human ideal is a Family of Love. We never succeed wholly in what we try to do in our families, but at least we have a *chance*, which is something we seldom have in connection with larger and more complex human institutions. Within the family we can count on a high degree of true affection and of desire to make the experiment succeed.

There are two societies known to man which serve the redemptive purpose better than others. One of these is the church and the other is the family. Among the many reasons for the manifest power of early Christianity was the substantial union of these two societies. In the Biblical phrase "the church in the house," the two societies on which we must depend are brought substantially together. Moffatt's translation, at the end of the fifth chapter of Acts, makes the partnership perfectly clear, but rightly reserves the reference to the home as the climax. The disciples, though beaten and warned against further witness, continued, without a break, to spread the message in the temple and at home.

Though we do not usually think of it in this connection, the Christian family is best understood in the light of the entire Christian emphasis on the power of the redemptive group. The philosophy of the family involves not merely biological necessity for human survival, but, far more, the entire Christian philosophy of how redemption takes place. The most common redemptive fellowship is not a prayer group in a church or a factory, but a family in which one man and one woman and children, for whom they are jointly responsible, provide us with the best foretaste of the

Kingdom of God that we know on this earth. We are thrilled when we hear of the growth of new prayer groups, but these are as nothing compared to the homes in even a small community. If we count the family units, as we ought, there are millions of redemptive fellowships in existence.

The family is the custodian and the only true example of life's highest known ideal. It is the one institution in which it is possible to say "we" without any loss of individuality. It is each for all and all for each, as is never the case in a secular society and seldom in a religious society. To say "we" and to mean it, is a very great spiritual achievement for the nominative plural is the noblest of the personal pronouns. A family in which each does what he can and each receives what he needs, wholly without financial calculation of earning or merit, represents the highest known ideal, our only true approximation to the Kingdom of God, yet countless humble families, made up of fallible persons, demonstrate this ideal in great measure every day of their lives. This is a foretaste of what the world ought to become. The categorical imperative for every family is this: So act that the fellowship of the family becomes an advance demonstration of the heavenly kingdom.

The secular atomism of the modern family makes three fundamental mistakes. First, it sees marriage as mere contract, second, it understands marriage as a private affair, and third, it adopts a philosophy of self-expression and empty freedom which rules out the claims of self-sacrifice and self-control.

As marriage becomes less sacred, and divorce more acceptable, many reach the facile conclusion that easy divorce is thereby justified. This is akin to the curious reasoning based on the Kinsey Report of sexual behavior, to the effect that infractions of the moral code are no longer evil because many commit them. But what a curiously naïve logic to conclude that right and wrong can be discovered by statistical method. Homosexual practices are not justified by the revelation, which nobody doubted, that a good many persons have temptations in this direction. What is commonly practiced is often wrong, in spite of its popularity.

Another phase of the moral problem of the family concerns the attitude of children toward their parents. The revolt against parental authority has gone so far that many young people have lost both politeness and a sense of respect. A characteristic college boy, when he heard the phrase "elders and betters," replied, "I have no betters." This superficial notion of equality where equality does not exist is the logical result of the doctrine of empty freedom, according to which each person is encouraged to follow self-expression and resist any limitation on personal decision. Naturally the family suffers first in this situation since the major values of family life, whether we realize it or not, depend upon a great degree of limitation on the personal action of the individual. The doctrine of freedom as popularly held and sometimes practiced leads not only to easy divorce, when marriage becomes galling, but likewise to a refusal, on the part of the children, to accept the responsibilities which membership entails. Insofar as freedom of action is seen as the primary or sole value, the family is progressively atomized and consequently destroyed.

We know a great deal about our diseased time when we see the growth of interest in abnormal psychology. In many universities the courses in abnormal behavior are the most popular of all courses in psychology, while numerous marriage courses achieve popularity because of their reputation for emphasis on sex. Apparently the undisguised pornography of the books in the drug stores is not sufficient to satisfy the demand. But what widespread futility there must be which causes people to turn to such substitutes! The bizarre interests are symptoms of a deep failure to find something positive and satisfying at the center of our lives.

A contemporary notion that is almost as popular as it is

absurd is the belief that the good life can be produced by the simple expedient of spreading sex knowledge. The fatuousness of this belief ought to be obvious when we reflect upon the fact that some of the most ruthless of sexual offenders are those whose sexual information must be immense. More than knowledge is necessary for the good life, whatever the area of experience. Knowledge is *necessary*, but it certainly is not *sufficient*.

It is likewise not enough to go to the other extreme and take a stiff line in regard to the remarriage of divorced persons. This is only one incident in a larger whole. What we need is a far wider view in which we refuse to concentrate merely on the relations of husband and wife and give our attention even more to the relations between parent and child. We make much of the break of affection which leads to divorce, but we have not given adequate attention to the break between parents and children, for which there is no handy common noun. What we need is an ideological transformation in regard to the family, including a new sense of motivation.

Fortunately, there are still thousands, perhaps millions of good families in America where the bonds of affection are kept strong, but not even these are free from the danger of the withering processes around them. Only by vigilance can the valued life we already have be kept and only by careful thought can its scope be increased. As the major threat to the life of the family lies in our ideas and convictions, so it is in this same area that our hope for a better future likewise lies. Can we recover or produce a conception of family life so intrinsically appealing that it makes us dissatisfied with the withering of the family in either the Russian or the Western style?

The chain of disaster is clear. The homes devoid of regular or continuous care lead directly to insecurity and delinquency on the part of the young. These in turn set up homes where a similar pattern is demonstrated. How shall we break this vicious chain? Before we can break it we need to know the nature of the trouble. Part of the trouble is, of course, economic, but by no means all. A good share of the trouble is moral and, if we go beyond the surface, most of it may be. One of the chief reasons why so many habitations are not homes is that other things are prized more.

The moral aspect of the decay of family life is obvious in the relations of the sexes to each other. There are, of course, millions of families in which there is lifelong marital fidelity, but it is frightening to realize that these may now constitute a minority of our population. If the figures given out by the Kinsey Report are reliable, it may be estimated that more than half the adult population of contemporary American shows, in practice, only slight respect for marital fidelity. What seems to have occurred is that great numbers consider sexual morality something quaint and meaningless for our time. Like the Russians in the first flush of the Revolution, many accept the "drink of water" conception and believe adultery a trivial affair, especially in the light of the fact that modern inventions make unlikely the permanent effects that have sometimes served as deterrents in the past.

Part of the trouble lies in the fact that so much of the idea of sanctity is gone. Easy divorce and quick remarriage, after the Nevada model, mean that marriage is seen primarily as a private convenience rather than a sacred undertaking. It ought to be clear that the present withering of the family is exactly what we should expect in the light of the absence of a generally accepted philosophy which would support the sanctity of marriage. The people who rush to Reno are not doing the surprising thing; they are doing the wholly natural thing, given their presuppositions.

The sacredness of marriage as it has been developed in the Judeo-Christian pattern of human life is best understood by emphasis on three main features. *The first of these is the notion of commitment as against mere contract.* The point that marriage is more than a contract needs to be given the widest possible dissemination, because many marriages owe their failure to a misunderstanding of this point. The first essential of marriage is the advance acceptance of the family relationship as *unconditional.* The father's responsibility to the child does not depend upon the child's health, his success or his character. The two participants in the marriage service pledge themselves, "for better and for worse." Frankly recognizing the dangers and pitfalls in advance, our religion tends to be intensely realistic rather than sentimental. The standardized service recognizes the strong possibility of economic difficulties, including real poverty, so the participants may take each other "for richer, for poorer." One partner may become ill, one may be unable to become a parent, but this eventuality is recognized too; they take each other "in sickness and in health." Far from being a temporary affair, we pledge our troth "so long as we both shall live." If it were a contract it would have an escape clause.

It is this mood of commitment which distinguishes the family from worldly institutions and makes it intrinsically a religious institution. Commitment is the crucial step in religious experience. Faith, we know, when we think about it, is not merely intellectual assent to a set of propositions, but the supreme gamble in which we stake our lives upon a conviction. It is closer to courage than it is to mere belief. In this profound sense, marriage is an act of faith. Undoubtedly some dim understanding of this is very widespread, even in our highly secularized society, and this accounts for the fact that so many, who have no connection at all with any organized religion, turn to the church when marriage is planned. They sense, somehow, that the highest things belong together; they are sufficiently sensitive to realize that there is at least one human undertaking that is debased if it is wholly secularized. We may be a pagan generation, but it is highly revealing that we are not willing to take our paganism straight.

The commitment we call marriage is not a bargain! It is a situation in which each gives *all* that he has, including all his devotion and all the fruits of his toil. "With *all* my worldly goods I thee endow." There is something extremely moving about the concept of *all*, as everyone recognizes when he reads the gospel story of the widow's mite. This is part of the reason why almost every marriage ceremony is profoundly moving. The charming young woman gives *all* to this young man. The result is that marriage is an amazing relation in which the ordinary rules of business, with its contracts and escape clauses and limited liabilities, are despised and set aside. Marriage is no marriage at all if it is conditional or partial or with the fingers crossed. There must be, on both sides, an uncalculating abandon, a mutual outpouring of love and loyalty in a prodigal way. The best-loved story of the New Testament is a family story, the story not primarily of the prodigal son, but of the father who was prodigal in his affection, and the story of every truly married couple is the story of the prodigal pair. The enduring rule of marriage is "Love one another with all your mind and heart and body." The truly married person, finite though he may be, is more interested in his mate's happiness than in his own, and his desire is to be to the other a constant delight. The fact that we do not achieve this ideal does not invalidate it.

The family is much older than our religion, and, as a natural grouping, would undoubtedly go on if our religion should come to an end, but the natural urges need a great deal of help and direction. The Judeo-Christian conception does not create the natural institution, but vastly improves it. It is like the Sabbath, in that it is a deliberate effort to facilitate holiness in the natural order. Marriage, as we have received it, is an attempt to produce a sanctuary out of a natural need. It is monogamy, but *monogamy plus*. It is the effort to make a holy path, not in separation from sex and work, or in seclusion, but in the midst of ordinary life. It thus maintains an ideal higher than that of the ascetic or monastic person. Marriage is the attempt to return man and woman to Paradise where they can live without sin. Such is our frailty, that this attempt does not wholly succeed, but the very effort is one of the noblest aspects of our common life. So long as marriage is seen as a holy commitment there is hope for our confused civilization.

The second main feature of marriage in the Judeo-Christian tradition is its public character. With one voice our best guides have told us that true marriage cannot be a private affair. Marriage is not primarily a device designed to provide personal pleasure to two people who pool their selfish interests. It is or can be a highly pleasurable undertaking, but the social responsibility involved in intrinsic. The union is likely to produce children who may be a burden or a strength to the outside community. It is therefore idle to tell the neighbors that it is none of their business. The family can never be a private institution because it contributes to the total good or ill of society; from it comes influence that affects mankind. The union of the parents of Abraham Lincoln affected millions besides themselves. In ancient Israel it was understood that the purposes of marriage were complex, rather than simple. It existed, they thought, to propagate the race, to satisfy emotional needs in beneficent ways and to perpetuate religious experience. In short, the family was understood as the fundamental unit of the social order.

The public significance of marriage has led to the formation of laws concerning both its establishment and its nullification. The common assumption of all such laws is that private or secret marriage is a contradiction in terms and quick marriage is always a failure to appreciate the total situation. The reason is that the community has a stake in the new union. A man and woman who begin living together with no further ado are outside the Judeo-Christian pattern because they are thereby denying the deep fact of community sharing. What we hold is that marriage, being intrinsically sacred, ought not to be consummated lightly, but should receive the blessing of a group who care. A wedding is a religious occasion during which a man and a woman make vows of lifelong fidelity, in the presence of those whose approbation they prize and whose blessing they seek . . .

At the Council of Trent much was made of the principle of *Proprius parochus,* the essence of this being the idea that, whenever possible, marriage is to be conducted in the parish of domicile. The purpose of the advice is that the judgment of local relatives, neighbors and clergy may thereby have more influence on the marriage. People care, and ought to care, about their reputations, among those with whom they work and live. That is why divorce comes about so much more easily in uprooted people. In the standard Quaker practice the couple intending marriage must seek the judgment of the local group to which they belong at least a month before the ceremony is performed. The Christian conscience has been consistently opposed to the existence of Gretna Greens, where runaway and secret marriages are made easy to the partners and profitable to the officials.

The third essential feature of marriage, in the Judeo-Christian tradition, is the free acceptance of a bond, something which limits the undisciplined self-expression which is natural to man. Just as marriage is not primarily for the personal pleasure of the couple concerned, likewise it is not compatible with absolute freedom. To the degree that the full freedom of expression and action are primary to the code of modern man, our basic conception of marriage is endangered. The man who understands marriage is not thereby made blind to the physical attractiveness of women other than his wife, but the possibility of making love to them is ruled out in advance. One big decision makes a host of minor decisions unnecessary. Free love, like private marriage, is a contradiction in terms, for conjugal love in many directions is real love in none.

Personal happiness must never become our chief end and goal. The purpose is not to be happy, but to perpetuate what is best for human life. Of course happiness usually comes in such a procedure, but it comes as a by-product. Emerson says wisely that the beauty of the sunrise or sunset is greatest when it comes as a surprise by the way. It is one lesson of the history of philosophical thought that the only way to *get* happiness is to *forget* it. Just as our popular philosophy is ambiguous about happiness it is likewise ambiguous about self-expression. Just what do we mean by it? *Which* side of ourselves do we propose to express? The idea of self-expression does not really help us, since the beastly side can be expressed just as the potential nobility can be expressed. Anyone who expressed all his thoughts and obeyed all his impulses would surely reveal himself as an utter fool.

The binding element is inherent in the family idea because without it, all the finer fruits of family love are impossible to produce. Marriage ties are permanently binding, not because a priest has said some words, but because an unbinding marriage is no marriage at all. The man who flits from one mate to another never really has *any*. But the central paradox is that he is bound thereby achieves the highest level of freedom; he is free from the superficiality of the philanderer.

The secularization of marriage, whether in the court house, the marriage parlor or the church, is a barometer of civilization. The enormous increase in divorce indicates the degree to which marriage has been looked upon as a contractual rather than a sacramental relation. This helps us to know where to put our emphasis if we care about the revival or continuance of commitment, should be lost by any generation, it would be exceedingly difficult to reproduce it. Without marriage in the sense of lifelong fidelity and mutual parental responsibility, the race would undoubtedly go on, but there is little likelihood that it would go on well. There would still be mating and there would still be children, but the most precious of intangibles would be lost. To recognize this is to understand something of our task.

Our present task is to help as many young persons as possible to a true understanding of marriage and to its continuing possibilities. They will be helped if they realize that marriage, not only on the wedding day, but in its entire course, is a public affair. If we take seriously the essentially public nature of marriage, the clear implication is that we must give the encompassing community a larger share in the undertaking. The chief way in which this may be done is by seeking the approval of the worshiping community well in advance. A step in this direction is the announcement of intentions or publishing of bans. Where this is required the sudden midnight ceremony in the house of a stranger is, of course, impossible. The experience of the Society of Friends, during the last three hundred years, may be profitable to other groups at this point. In a Quaker wedding the stake of the entire group is recognized from the beginning in that the couple intending marriage bring forth their proposal to a monthly meeting of their fellow members. If the union seems, under a sense of divine guidance, to be in good order, the marriage is allowed and a date set for it. Usually time is given for a committee to present a report a month later, so that a sudden wedding is impossible. When the day of the wedding arrives, the couple say their vows of fidelity before their friends and fellow members, a number of whom sign the certificate as having witnessed the vows. Thus there is no need of a clergyman or officiating minister. The conviction is that there is nothing which such a person could add, for the central fact has already occurred. The public nature of marriage is taken so seriously that the stamp of approval is that, not of one man, but of the group itself. That such an experience often reaches great heights of reverence and high seriousness goes without saying. But something of this character can also be caught by others who follow different procedures.

The simplicity and directness of the Quaker marriage vows, as they arise spontaneously out of a setting of profound silence may also be a model for others. "In the presence of the Lord and before these friends, I, John, take thee Mary, to be my wife, promising, with divine assistance, to be unto thee a loving and faithful husband so long as we both shall live." Whether this or the vow found in the *Book of Common Prayer* is used, there is little doubt that any marriage service is deepened if the bride and groom learn their own vows and say them without prompting. This takes us one step farther away from the banal "I do" and provides something beautiful to remember and repeat in subsequent days. Moreover the mutual task of learning the vows in advance is a beneficent experience. *It is beneficent because it extends the period during which the couple are made conscious of the religious aspect of their union.*

Men and women who are joined in wedlock according to the *Book of Common Prayer* are reminded, during the public service itself, that the normal expectation of their union is children, and that the coming of such children will involve their parents in a solemn responsibility for their care. Only the prudish think this indelicate. Not all people who marry are *able* to have children, but marriage without the *hope* of children is no marriage. Couples who value inordinately their own ease, who wish to sleep all night without the disturbance of infants, and who desire to keep their homes in perfect order, naturally fear the introduction of children into their lives, and some resist their coming for these reasons. But these are never really good homes, even though they may be orderly and neat in outward appearance. Frequently such homes go on the rocks of internal discord and this is what we ought to expect, since love of ease is a weak human bond. As men and women grow older, losing some of their physical attractiveness, their lives need powerful connecting links, and the most powerful of all human links is children who belong to both and who have been brought into existence through the mutual love of both parents. One of the really encouraging signs of our time is the fact that so many young people, when approaching marriage, now talk frankly, though not lightly, of their hope of children.

Throughout all of our known history, birth has been looked upon as a religious event. Life is full of crises, but man seems to have realized early that a crisis may be a means of divine revelation. Birth and death are such crises, and they are equally mystifying. The notion of an end is solemn, but the notion of a beginning is equally solemn. Once there was not this new person at all, and now he is alive, with years of varied experience before him. He is a unique combination of factors, never seen in the world before and this tiny body is destined to be intertwined with a responsible soul, capable of knowing God and sensitive to the call of duty. If a sacrament is a way of intertwining the material and the spiritual so that new grace emerges, the birth of any baby is surely sacramental for all who can appreciate it.

All sensitive parents realize that their baby is a sheer gift. They have had, nine months earlier, some small part in the production of the tiny body, but this seems almost trivial in relationship to the entire event. Fathers and mothers cannot *make* a life; at best they can be instruments of its emergence. We can help, in minor ways, to provide a good physical environment, including nourishment, but we cannot make anything *grow*. We cannot even heal; the best that we can do in this regard is to try to eliminate some of the factors which hinder or retard the healing process, which is something *given*. Accordingly the wise parents look at the little bundle of flesh and say to themselves that this is really a little stranger. He isn't even *theirs*, though he is their responsibility for a few years. They are given the high privilege of guiding his life, protecting him from various dangers and watching him develop into a true man. Adequate recognition of this makes the crisis called birth not merely a natural event, but a religious event also. To be allowed to guide the life of a child is to be given an *incredible compliment*. It means that we are trusted with the responsibility of forming characters which may have eternal significance. No sensitive person can face this relationship without a deep sense of unworthiness as well as of honest reverence.

Even when the Christian faith is well taught in churches, it must be supplemented in homes. This can be done by parents working alone or in groups. Some of the most promising of contemporary experiments are devoted to domestic group teaching, thus producing the church that is in the house. This identification of the home and the faith involves a great psychological advantage. There is always a danger that children will think of religion as something confined to a special building with a special kind of architecture, and appropriate only for special days. Much of this danger is avoided if the study of the Bible or of Christian history is conducted on a weekday in an ordinary house which is a center of living and loving and working. The church building and the domestic building need not be rivals for the affectionate interest of the young, but can serve complementary purposes.

We need to use all of the imagination we can muster to think how to make prayer, which is the heart of true religion, real in our homes. Certainly we want to avoid the mistake of allowing it to seem burdensome or forbidding, with the sad consequence that independent young minds rebel. If we are to avoid this outcome it is necessary to keep our religion gay and as natural as eating or sleeping. No doubt the best practice is to see to it that every meal, in which the whole family participates, begins with a time of reverence. Here variety, within the general pattern, is a help. Sometimes we should sing, sometimes we should pray in silence, sometimes there should be the use of classic prayers, sometimes there should be spontaneous prayers on the part of members of different ages. Above all we should not be self-conscious about praying in the presence of one another. We are failing if we cannot make the experience of thanking God as natural and as wholesome as the experience of telling one another of our love and admiration. When we recognize the incredible compliment that God has paid us in allowing us to influence, in such measure, the lives of growing human beings, prayer is the only normal response. All of the major occasions in family life, whether birthdays or anniversaries or starting to school or marriage, are of such intrinsic importance that they become occasions for prayer whenever the Christian religion is taken seriously.

Each home will have to make its own experiment in religious education if the moral sag of our time is to be altered. The change cannot come by governmental fiat or even by some public educational reform. The best education is that of the laboratory and the only laboratory in which the most important lessons can be learned is that of the separated home. Some of these, such as that of the British Royal Family, can make a great difference in our civilization. There is no way to overestimate the beneficent moral effect which Queen Elizabeth and her family are having, not merely for England and the whole British Commonwealth, but for the entire Western world. Here, at the focus of admiring attention, is a scene of family happiness and fidelity which makes the too common café society of our time seem utterly shoddy by contrast. The center of attention is a really good young family, marked by fidelity, and this is a moral force beyond price.

Each little family may exert its own influence, on a smaller scale, even though it is not the center of general attention. It is sobering to go through the country by car or train and begin to contemplate the meaning of all the little houses. In most of these homes dwell one man and one woman and their little ones, all working together to achieve an honorable life. Their success almost never appears in newspapers, but perhaps it is better thus. Each little unit is striving to pay its bills, get rid of the mortgage, keep the grass cut, keep the children fed and clothed, buy new shoes, and send the children to school with regularity. No national scheme we could imagine would provide the same drive that is provided by the combination of the individual pride and affection of all these families existing separately, *each as a little kingdom.* In the larger community action is difficult and often slow, but in a good family there is wonderful freedom to act. Here are both initiative and independence which make the American home the bulwark of the American way. It is a good way and it will survive. We must keep the private home and we must make it better. If we have enough good homes we shall have a good world. But we shall not succeed in making them better in time unless we have the kind of motivation which a crusade makes possible. The problems of family life today are so great that they cannot possibly be solved on the merely secular level. Only something as strong as a sense of religious vocation will suffice.

If the hard-pressed men and women in the little homes, who are faced with difficulties every day, can be made to feel that they, in maintaining families, are in a crucial position, doing that which the world sorely needs and without which the world will go to pieces, they may be enabled to face their tasks with a wholly new spirit. It is the responsibility of every reader of this book to feel this sense of vocation in trying to make his own home into a place where the Christian revolution begins, and to spread this idea to as many others as possible.

The individual home, with its beds and games and dining table and books, may seem a tiny thing in contrast to states and governments and armies; but it is by means of such tiny things that the world is changed. The home may, like the mustard seed, be the least of all the seeds; but seed it undoubtedly is. If we could have enough really good homes, we should have a very different world; and we are not likely to have a good world without them.

The good homes do not come by accident. It is undoubtedly true that there are good homes, marked by deep and enduring affection, in which there is no conscious Christian emphasis at all, but there is a greater likelihood of success in these matters if there is a uniting faith at the center. Ordinarily we love each other better if we love God first. The best affection comes as a by-product when noble things are attempted and done together. "Life has taught us," wrote Exupery, "that love does not consist in gazing at each other, but in looking outward together in the same direction."

The late Henry T. Hodgkin helped many of us by his comparison of the home to an island. He pointed out in *The Christian Revolution* that our modern continents emerged originally from the sea as separated islands, which were really the tops of mountains. The continents grew by the increase in the number of these islands. Each home, Dr. Hodgkin believed, can be a small island which is a truly manageable unit. We cannot change the whole world at once; we cannot alter greatly a political party or a labor union, or even a local church; each of these is too much for us. But, in the little island, which we call home, we can set the conditions to a remarkable degree. This is where each is able to make a radical difference. This is how the world can be changed.

Selections in Chapter Six are taken from:
The Common Ventures of Life
The Yoke of Christ
The Recovery of Family Life

Chapter Seven

THE
UNIVERSAL MINISTRY

A new and exciting emphasis which is now becoming an important aspect of today's New Reformation, is the concept of the universal ministry. This theme has been close to Elton Trueblood's heart for forty-three years, ever since his first book, **The Essence Of Spiritual Religion,** wherein he devoted a chapter to the topic, "The Abolition Of The Laity." Dr. Trueblood believes that the words "Christian" and "minister" are synonymous, and in this chapter he shares with his readers why he believes contemporary Christians must recover an understanding of the universal ministry if renewal in the church is to become a reality.

J.R.N.

What we need is a radical change of some kind. The parable that applies to one situation is the contemporary parable of the *big dose*, according to which some of the modern wonder drugs must be given in very large amounts in order for them to make a *sufficient* difference. Often the small dose is entirely wasted, because the body adjusts rapidly to it. In some medication, if we do not give a large dose, we might as well give none. Not only must the dose be big; it must also be new. The reason for this is that so many have already failed to be moved by present means. We have done about all we can do unless we find a new approach. It must be an approach which gives a practical means of service to the many humble people who are really eager to help, but do not now know what to do. There is actually a great deal of good will and a vast store of decency, but the problem is to harness this good will in some effective manner. In nearly every community there are hundreds of people who are sincerely eager to do something to help to produce a better world, but they do not know what to do. All of the problems seem so large that any effort appears futile and therefore nothing is done. What we need is a *handle*. Where can it be found?

So far as the Christian faith is concerned the practical handle in our time is lay religion. If in the average church we should suddenly take seriously the notion that every lay member, man or woman, is really a minister of Christ, we could have something like a revolution in a very short time; it would constitute the big dose and the required novelty. Suddenly the number of ministers in the average church would jump from *one* to *five hundred*. This is the way to employ valuable but largely wasted human resources. The change that could come in the visitation of new families, in the spoken and written word, and in public witness might be incalculably great. In a few communities, where the idea has been seriously tried, the change has already been encouragingly great.

Let no one have the temerity to say that this is what we

already have. It is not! There are thousands of contemporary churches in which nothing of the kind is even *understood*, let alone demonstrated. Most Protestants pay lip service to the Reformation doctrine of the priesthood of every believer, but they do not thereby mean to say that every Christian is a minister. Many hasten to add that all they mean by the familiar doctrine is that nobody needs to confess to a priest, since each can confess directly to God. The notion that this doctrine erases the distinction between laymen and minister is seldom presented seriously, and would, to some, be shocking, but it does not take much study of the New Testament to realize that the early Christians actually operated on this revolutionary basis.

How far we have departed from the New Testament practice may be shown by describing a contemporary Christian gathering, the example being taken almost at random. The gathering was organized to strengthen the Protestant forces of the city, a speaker being brought from a distance. The entire affair was conducted by the local ministerial association, one pastor giving the invocation, one reading the Scripture, another praying before the offering, a fourth introducing the speaker and a fifth giving the benediction. The whole service was practically identical with that which most of the attenders had experienced earlier the same day, except that the professional participants were now more numerous. There was no surprise, no novelty, no real beauty or dignity, and consequently very little attention. It was as though an old record, worn by much use, were being run again and no one seemed to have any clear reason for running it. The hymns were sung, not because some great testimony was being jointly made, but because hymn singing was the conventional thing to do, and the prayers were given, not because of inner compulsion, but because praying was expected.

On the platform all were professionals. There was not a layman, not a woman, not a young person. In the congregation sat about two hundred people, *one* of whom was possibly under twenty-one years of age! This seems shocking, and means defeat, but why should we consider it surprising? What was there to draw the young or the adventurous? Even if they *had* been present, they would have been expected to play the role of spectators or mere audience, watching the professionals perform. Thus the mood of the spectator, which is so destructive of any vital movement, is actually encouraged.

The First Reformation which came to its climax more than three centuries ago produced a great new power, by something analagous to a change of gears. As we look back now on that marvelous and rapid development, which did so much to bring democracy to our world, we realize that the crucial step was that of making available the open Bible. That is why, so far as the English-speaking world is concerned, the key date is 1611. In the intervening three hundred and forty years we have come to take so much for granted the availability of the Bible to the ordinary Christian that we have little understanding how different life was when the Bible was available only to the learned, and to the priestly caste. The Bible, being a revolutionary document, is naturally an instrument of emancipation. The men and women, who could read the Bible for themselves and thus begin to understand God's will directly, soon developed a radical democracy in church government, and, once they had experience in democratic church government, they were not satisfied without democracy in secular government. Thus democratic practices arose simultaneously on two sides of the Atlantic in the small devout communities, especially those of the nonconformist variety.

Now, after more than three centuries, we can, if we will, change gears again. Our opportunity *for a big step lies in opening the ministry to the ordinary Christian in much the same manner that our ancestors opened Bible reading to the ordinary Christian.* To do this means, in one sense, the inauguration of a new Reformation while in another it means the logical completion of the earlier Reformation in which the implications of the position taken were neither fully understood nor loyally followed.

There have been different great steps at different times in Christian history, because one of the most remarkable features of the Christian faith is its ability to reform itself *from the inside*. However vigorous the outside critics of the Church may be, the inside critics, who love the movement which they criticize, are far more vigorous and searching. Reformation is not accidental or exceptional, but characteristic and intrinsic. The crust forms repeatedly, but there is always a volcanic power to break through it.

In the nineteenth century the Church experienced a marvelous reformation in the sudden and explosive growth of the missionary movement. Many aspects of Christian life were radically changed in this way and young people went out by the thousands to the ends of the earth. This was a proud and glorious chapter in Christian history and it is by no means ended, but the first impact of this movement is over. Indeed, after years of expansion, we have suffered *reverses*. We still sing, "Jesus shall reign," but we are well aware that the missionary movement now faces terrible obstacles, particularly in China, where most of the Western workers are not allowed to remain and where many of the Chinese converts have, under heavy pressure, renounced the faith they once espoused.

Now, just as one great chapter of expansion is temporarily ended, another chapter is being inaugurated. This is the chapter devoted to the ministry of the laity. Whether or not this will produce a new reformation we cannot yet know, but we do know that, as has been true in earlier movements, almost identical developments are occurring spontaneously and without knowledge of one another, in a great many different localities. The great Church Congress of Germany, which brought together almost four hundred thousand persons in Berlin in the summer of 1951, was largely inspired by the concept of lay religion and largely organized by a layman, Reinold von Thadden, whose work for the promotion of lay religion has been honored in America. Many conferences on lay religion have been held in 1952 and more are already planned for succeeding years. We have witnessed the organization of "United Church Men," the beginnings of a training school for lay ministers, the spread of the Christopher Movement among Roman Catholics, the growing use of the Yoke-pin, the organization of Presbyterian Men, and much more. Every succeeding week brings new evidence of the vitality of an idea whose time has come.

A quarter century ago the most commonly quoted remark of a contemporary Christian was the statement of Archbishop William Temple about the great new fact of our time. The great new fact, this wise man said, was the growing union in the churches. Undoubtedly the words were accurate when they were first spoken, but they would not be accurate if spoken now. Today we can still be grateful for the amount of church union that has been accomplished, but it is no longer novel and it is no longer the matter of first importance in Christian strategy. The great new fact in Christian experience today is the powerful drive in developing a universal ministry. We have made a brave start on the abolition of the laity, a movement according to which all who are Christians, whatever their particular gifts, must be engaged in some kind of ministry.

The old-fashioned idea, which we are now trying so hard to overcome, was the idea that religion is a professional matter. In spite of the current emphasis on lay religion there are people who, when they think of religion, immediately think of priests or clergymen or theologians. Religion, they tend to suppose, is something that preachers have. If a man becomes deeply interested in the effort to make the gospel prevail, they begin to suspect that he has a professional stake in the religion business. There are people who leave religious discussion to their priests, much as they leave medical discussion to their physicians. Religion, then, is like medicine. There is a sense in which both are good for everybody, but they are dangerous in both instances, unless they are administered by those who have the professional stamp upon them. The very phrase "enter the church" has sometimes meant to become a clergyman. The lay member, of course, has his own responsibilities, but they are of a minor nature. Sometimes it seems that his major responsibilities are merely to add himself to the listening congregation and to give some money to support the work of the pastor.

It is obvious that there are many people who enjoy this sharp division of labor in the religious view; it is so much easier to sit in the balcony than to act on the stage. Life is far simpler if we are not required to participate. The layman who leaves all major responsibilities of the church to his pastor is really in a very comfortable position. He can tend to his secular business with very little interference from religious considerations. He can leave to the pastor, not only all of the preaching and praying, but also all of the visiting of new people. He is then free to criticize, if things are not well done, and he has an easy conscience because he has no important task in which it is possible to fail.

However comfortable and convenient this balcony view of the lay member has been, it is now conspicuously out of date and, in any case, betrays a complete misunderstanding of the nature of the Christian cause. Early Christianity was, for the most part, a movement in which the distinction between clergy and laity was utterly unknown. Indeed, our conventional distinction between clerical and lay Christians does not appear anywhere in the entire New Testament. There was, at first, nothing which even approached the separated priesthood. The distinction broke down on both sides. On what we might call the professional side, it broke down because a man like Paul worked with his own hands. "For you remember our labor and toil; we worked night and day, that we might not burden any of you, while we preached to you the gospel of God" (1 Thess. 2:9). On what we are tempted to call the lay side, ordinary men and women worked mightily to extend Christ's Kingdom. Early Christianity won against great odds, not primarily because it had a few brilliant leaders, but far more because the idea of a nonministering Christian seems to have been rejected unanimously. *The mood was not so much anti-clerical as anti-lay*. Insofar as we are trying to abolish the laity, we are, in essence, trying to recapture the mood of first-century Christianity.

How little, in primitive Christianity, the call to ministry was limited to an especially ordained group is obvious from the careful study of the New Testament epistles. For example, we read in II Corinthians 5:18, "And all things are of God, who hath reconciled us to Himself by Jesus Christ, and hath given to us the ministry of reconciliation." The word "us" is used with the same denotation in both parts of the sentence and the first clearly refers to *all Christians*, since it is not a special class that God has reconciled. Therefore the second use, in regard to the ministry, must also refer to all. The original recipients of the epistle, i.e., "all the saints that are in Achaia," are urged to comport themselves so as to bring no bad reputation on the ministry (II Corinthians 6:3).

This acceptance of the ministry of all, in a radical democracy, did not, so far as early Christians were concerned, involve a dull uniformity or any lack of a division of labor. Like all intelligent democrats, the early Christians understood thoroughly that democracy is compatible with responsible leadership. The formula developed was that, while all are called to be ministers, some are particularly called to be pastors. It is a mark of our present failure even to understand the New Testament conception, that we ordinarily use the words "pastor" and "minister" synonymously or interchangeably.

The mature statement of the primitive Christian pattern of the ministry is given in the fourth chapter of Ephesians. In this statement, an amplification of that in I Corinthians 12:28 ff., there is a frank recognition of a division of labor without any denial of the universality of responsibility. We are missing the early Christian conception, either when we so stress the ministry of all that we neglect the importance of the pastoral office or when we so stress the importance of the pastoral office that we deny the ministry of all. The mature statement in Ephesians upholds the necessity of responsible leadership, but the significant factor is the understanding of the function of the leader. *His function is to help to equip the members for the work of the ministry.* The good pastor or teacher is one who cultivates the ministerial possibilities of his fellow members.

A full understanding of this primitive Christian pattern, which proved to be enormously successful, will avoid many dangers in the *release* of new lay forces in our time. It is unfortunately true that there are a few clergymen who resist the fuller participation of laymen in the ministry, because they feel that their own function thereby seems less important, in that they no longer have a monopoly on the work of the ministry. But it is important to report that the pastors who resist the return to the primitive Christian pattern, out of a desire to hold jealously to their position, are really very few. There are, indeed, some who frankly admit that they do not want laymen to preach, because they look upon the pulpit as their special area of competence and they do not wish to miss any opportunity to use it, but these constitute only a small minority. The average pastor, at least in America, is a highly democratic person and deeply committed to the idea set forth in this chapter. The real difficulty lies with the laymen rather than with the clergymen. Many clergymen hate to be called "Reverend" and do everything they can to resist the tendency to set them apart. It is not they, but the ordinary laymen who, in most instances, speak of men "of the cloth," and expect religious functions to be performed by persons of a professional class. If we are to change the situation we must change the attitudes of the laymen; the clergy are, for the most part, ready for a change now. Many pastors are embarrassed by the tendency to call on them for official prayers, and wish such opportunities could be more widely spread, but the pressure of convention is so great that most pastors acquiesce rather than act so as to cause trouble.

The existence of a large body of able and sincere pastors is one of the most hopeful factors in our present situation. If we can match them with still greater numbers of concerned laymen, men who are willing to break the religious conventions of the past, our time may be one of genuine hope. Good pastors need have no fear, since the basic Christian pattern of organization really ennobles, rather than degrades, the work of the pastor or teacher. He is successful, not insofar as he makes men depend upon him, but rather insofar as he can help them to make their own religious lives strong. Ordinarily a man is not a good pastor unless his influence is infectious or highly multiplying. The really successful preacher will have those who have heard him clamoring for opportunities to preach. A religion that is not contagious is not genuine.

The more we study the early Church the more we realize that it was a society of ministers. About the only similarity between the Church at Corinth and a contemporary congregation, either Roman Catholic or Protestant, is that both are marked, to a great degree, by the presence of sinners. After that the similarity ends, for we think it is normal for one man to do all the preaching, while the others are audience, whereas in Corinth, many did the preaching. "When you come together," reported their most famous visitor, "each one has a hymn, a lesson, a revelation, a tongue, or an interpretation" (I Cor. 14:26).

The ministry of original Christianity was one of its most

revolutionary aspects. In contrast to all previous models, the new fellowship emerged as a dynamic force without priest or rabbi or medicine man. Since the one form of leadership which was retained, glorified and universalized was the prophetic one, the pattern, both in terms of what it included and what it excluded, was essentially new. The Gospel, so far as the history of religion is concerned, represented the emergence of genuine novelty, the emerging pattern rejecting both the lay and the clerical ideal. Though Christians accepted the necessity of leadership, the actual leadership was not sacerdotal. This explains, in some measure, why the faith was so mystifying to observers, whether Jew or Greek; it did not conform to any known pattern of religious behavior. Thus there is no real surprise in the fact that the observers were sufficiently puzzled to say, "You bring some strange things to our ears" (Acts 17:20).

There is always a temptation to suppose that the early Christian emphasis required them or requires now a denial of differences in function. Why not say that all Christians are supposed to be ministers and leave it at that? Why not deny the need of pastors at all? The earliest Christians were far too realistic to fall into this trap, because they saw that, if the ideal of universal ministry is to be approximated at all, there must be some people who are working at the job of bringing this highly desirable result to pass. The disciples had the word of Christ about the necessity of laborers, if the harvest was to be rightly handled, and they knew that no grain harvests itself! According to the Gospel record, Christ twice commanded his followers to pray for the emergence of a labor force, which was the obvious bottleneck of the new movement. The harvest, i.e., the development of a redemptive fellowship made up wholly of ministers, is potentially great, but it cannot be actualized without the labor of men who are sufficiently gifted and dedicated to facilitate its accomplishment.

The New Testament pattern, then, involves, both a generalized and a particular ministry. When the Apostle

Paul uses the term pastor he equates it with teacher and makes it very clear that this is by no means the whole conception of the ministry. The ministry is for all who are called to share in Christ's life, but the pastorate is for those who possess the peculiar gift of being able to help other men and women to practice any ministry to which they are called. The classic passage which, fortunately, is becoming more and more familiar to literate contemporary Christians, develops the pattern which we have come to call The Equipping Ministry. "And these were his gifts: some to be . . . pastors and teachers, to equip God's people for work in his service" (Eph. 4:12, NEB).

The idea of the pastor as the equipper is one which is full of promise, bringing back self-respect to men in the ministry when they are sorely discouraged by the conventional pattern. Here is a job which is intrinsically hard, as the job of the official prayer at banquets is intrinsically easy. To watch for underdeveloped powers, to draw them out, to bring potency to actuality in human lives—this is a self-validating task. A man who knows that he is performing such a function is not bothered by problems of popular acceptance because he is working at something which he can respect. With self-respect he can bear the attacks of his enemies and detractors with a certain confidence. Though his life is not easy, he is saved from triviality, for he knows that his work is both necessary and important, because the stakes, so far as civilization is concerned, are high. Because the task is itself ennobling, he need not worry whether he is called "Reverend" or "Doctor." The dignity of his life is involved, not in status, but in function.

One of the ways by which the image of the professional minister can be improved is that of a better linguistic designation. Language is often both a revelation of what men think and a barrier to improvement. To call a man who is engaged in the equipping ministry *the minister* of the congregation, as is now often done, is seen to be inept as soon as we examine the implication of such language. If Dr. Jones is *the* minister of the First Presbyterian Church of Centerville, it follows logically that the ordinary members are *not* ministers. And the shame is that this is exactly what many of them desire. It is clearly a neat device for people to hire someone to be their minister, thus relieving all of the ordinary members of ministerial responsibilities. But this way lies death, for there is no possibility of sustained or enlarged vitality without personal involvement, and personal involvement means ministry, if it means anything at all.

What then shall the equipper be called, if not the minister? Here we have real difficulty since all of the familiar terms have unacceptable overtones. "Elder" won't do for it sounds stuffy, and is as ridiculous when applied to a young man as is "Father" when applied to a bachelor. "Preacher," which was once conventional on the frontier, won't do for it refers to only one aspect, though an important one, of a complex function. In many ways "pastor" is best, partly because it is dignified by New Testament usage, but even more because it places emphasis upon the relationship to those who are being led. The Lutheran tradition has made zealous use of this term, with many good results, one of which is the avoidance of the temptation to make an indiscriminate and illicit use of the honorific "Doctor." In spite of these advantages, the word pastor implies much that we do not mean and ought not to mean. Sheep are not particularly productive, except in providing wool and mutton. Furthermore, sheep are notorious for their placidity while they are being led, but this is no part of the ideal of Christian men and women in the common ministry of common life. A man who supposes that his relationship to the members of a congregation is in any sense identical to the relationship between a shepherd and a flock is in for some big surprises. Another serious difficulty with pastoral terminology is that modern men have very little knowledge of the ways of sheep, some city dwellers never having seen a sheep in their whole lives. Here is a valid example of how language can become almost meaningless because of a radical change in manner of living.

Some are now coming to believe that the least inadequate

or distorting term for a spiritual leader in a congregation is "coach." This word has overtones which modern man comprehends very well, indeed. Furthermore, the image of the coach is one which can be universally honored by young and old alike. Everyone knows that, in the development of a football or a baseball team, the quality of the coaching staff often makes a crucial difference. With no essential change in the personnel of the players, the effectiveness of the team is sometimes changed radically when a new coach begins to operate. He sees that Smith can probably be shifted from guard to halfback and that the fullback, having never been used in defense, may have in him the possibility of becoming a successful line-backer.

The glory of the coach is that of being the discoverer, the developer, and the trainer of the powers of other men. But this is exactly what we mean when we use the Biblical terminology about the equipping ministry. A Christian society is made up of men and women whose powers in the ministry are largely unused because they are unsuspected. The Christian coach will be one who is more concerned, therefore, in developing others than in enhancing his own prestige. Ideally, he will not do anything himself, if another can be enabled to grow by being encouraged to do it. If the sermon can be given effectively by an ordinary member, the pastor, insofar as he is truly a coach, may keep silent while the other person may cost him far more in time and toil than his own preparation for speaking would have cost.

Since the equipping minister must not be above the heat of the battle, he is, ideally, not only a coach, but a "playing coach," sometimes carrying the ball himself and sometimes seeing to it that another carries it. Thus, he is both a minister and the encourager, a teacher and a developer of his fellow ministers, who are the members of the Church of Christ. The mark of his success is not the amount of attention which he can focus on himself, but the redemptive character which emerges in the entire congregation or team. Fundamentally, he is called to be a catalytic agent, often making a radical difference while being relatively inconspicuous. This is a high ideal. Indeed, it is an ideal so high that it can be made attractive to the very men who are repelled by the lower ideal which is the only one which some of them have hitherto known. Such an ideal, if generally accepted, can provide a practical starting point for the reconstruction of the Church. It is not the end of the matter, but is undoubtedly a viable beginning.

Though the early standard was not maintained in the Church, it is still valid. A full understanding of the Christian message leads us straight to the position that all Christians are ministers and that the mere layman is nonexistent. There may be some division of labor in this generalized ministry, as St. Paul explained, but we must not suppose that a division of labor necessarily entails a difference in rank or honor. There may be diversities of gifts, but there is the same Spirit.

The great ideal of the abolition of the laity has caught hold of men fitfully, but it has never been seriously followed in the Church at large, at least not since the first Christian century. Sometimes the cleavage has been so marked that one kind of doctrine has been held suitable for the priests who know and another has been taught to the common man. This is dangerous on the grounds of sincerity, if on no other, and certainly finds no counterpart in the teaching of Jesus. Spiritual religion is a religion of *veracity* and is willing to run the risks of truthtelling. If an educated minister does not believe in a physical hell, he is undermining the very foundation of faith when he proceeds to preach such a hell to his supposedly ignorant hearers. The abolition of the laity involves an abolition of a double standard of truth and a double standard of morality. The "hard sayings" of Jesus, which we find especially in the Sermon on the Mount, are shorn of their power if we interpret them as applicable to the priesthood and not to the common man.

That is too easy a way out of the difficulty and spiritual religion cannot take it.

The notion of a universal priesthood has broken out in many strange places in the history of the Church, thus showing that there is something about the nature of the Christian message which will not let men rest content with an easy acceptance of a two-level order. Among ordinary Christians there have long been practices which tend, in reality, to deny a sharp cleavage between clergy and laity, in spite of what they say. The practice of family prayer is a case in point. Countless Christian parents have been priests and priestesses at their own firesides, as have Hebrew parents for so many generations.

The ideal of the abolition of the laity came near to concrete embodiment at the time of the Reformation. Martin Luther envisaged the ideal for a time and made it his battle cry when he spoke of "the Priesthood of the Believer," but he seems to have made no serious attempt to put it into practice. As a matter of fact most Christians, unless their attention is called to this high ideal, consider that a few are ministers while most are not, and they mean by a minister a person who has had theological training or has had the rite of ordination. When we consider the question we quickly realize that this conception of the ministry is amazingly artificial. A man might go to a dozen theological schools and be well versed in Church History, and yet not be a person at all able to cultivate and arouse the spirit of worship in ordinary men. He might not even *care* to cultivate and arouse this spirit. The same can be said of any ceremonial act, such as ordination, with or without the laying on of hands. It is hard to see how the prophetic spirit can be inherited or passed on by mechanical arrangement. What we want, then, in spiritual religion is a conception of the ministry that accords with reality and is not merely a matter of externals that cannot possibly change the inner spirits of men.

Always, if we take the idea of the Universal Mission seriously, we must watch for unused human resources, because we are not rich enough to waste any. One of the major resources now largely unexploited is that of retired persons. In our present commercial society, the shortening of the work week is matched by the advancement of retirement to an earlier age. Consequently, an extended period of time is available for noncommercial employment. While some find that their retirement pay or social security is not sufficient for the cost of living and therefore seek paid employment after official retirement, there are many others who, with some care in management of funds, can be liberated entirely, for long periods, from the necessity of earning.

What the Church must do for retired Christians, if it is to accept the missionary conception of membership, is to equip people to make the retired years into years of glorious opportunity for service. For the committed Christian, retirement means not an introduction to nothingness, but liberation for service. If this idea is to be effective, we must begin preparation for liberation long before it occurs, because, if we wait, it may already be too late. That the idea is beginning to catch on is deeply encouraging. Recently, a man said, half-jokingly, "I am going as a missionary to Florida." Whether the freedom from toil, which modern technology makes possible, is a blessing or a curse depends, in large measure, upon the pattern of thinking about ourselves and our vocations. It is here that the Christian faith can make some of its most potent contributions. The man who always wanted to be a missionary, but could not do so, he thought, because of the demands of family and secular occupation, may bring deep meaning to his mature years by volunteering to engage in work for which there is no financial support. Assuming good health, which is increasingly experienced after the age of retirement, new and hitherto unsuspected avenues may open. Thereby the

Christian Movement may again demonstrate its genius for the creation of novelty.

Once we accept the idea that the field is the world, we change the whole image of the Mission. Much of the problem arises from the gratuitous assumption that the missionary is necessarily a clergyman and a man devoid of skills in common life, thus representing a pattern which is almost sure to seem obsolete in the modern world. But if we realize that missionary merely means any follower of Christ who takes his faith seriously, the whole undertaking is revolutionized.

An effort has been made to convince Christians that they are "ministers," whatever their occupation, but success in this effort is far from complete. People still speak of the clergyman as "the minister" which, of course, eliminates themselves from a similar function, since the definite article is intrinsically singular. While the change in semantics in regard to the sharp distinction between minister and lay Christian may be virtually impossible at this time, there appears to be a different situation in regard to the concept of Mission. In any case, this is an area of hope. If wide exposure is given to the idea that the Mission is essential to the Christian Cause and that it recognizes neither geographical nor professional limitations, a start has been made on the road to renewal.

Selections in Chapter Seven are taken from:
Your Other Vocation
The Yoke of Christ
The Incendiary Fellowship
The Essence of Spiritual Religion
The Validity of the Christian Mission

Chapter
Eight

THE
CHRISTIAN MISSION

*O*ver the years the Christian church has had difficulty defining what is meant by the word "mission." To most Christians it has a narrow meaning which can briefly be understood as the evangelization of people in another part of the world. Increasingly, however, Christians are realizing that this word has a much broader meaning. All persons who believe in Jesus Christ are called to be missionaries, and the witness to this faith has absolutely no geographical boundaries. In this chapter, Elton Trueblood clarifies for the sincere seeker what Christian mission is, and defends its purpose and goals.

J.R.N.

The Church of Jesus Christ does not *have missions;* in its very life it is *Mission*.

It is not *our* religion that we, as Christians, are required to share. It is *Christ's*. The moment we try to hold our faith in such a way that we keep it to ourselves, and make no effort to influence other people who might be liberated by it, we are showing that we have a complete misunderstanding of the situation."Any man who has a religion," said Robert E. Speer, "is bound to do one of two things with it, change it or spread it. If it is true, he must spread it." The present tendency to renounce the missionary movement, on the ground of tolerance of all faiths, is a sign not of advance but of intellectual confusion. A tolerance which blurs distinctions is no more valuable in religion that it is in science or any other realm. Concern for our fellow men does not mean leaving them to their own unaided devices, when a modest but courageous witness on our part could make a difference in their lives. The chief reason for the necessity of witness is the simple fact that thoughtful men are found to share what they truly prize. If the gospel is true, our responsibility is to help to make it prevail. There is no place in Christianity for mere well-wishers. The task of contemporary Christians is to get out of the balcony and onto the witness stand.

Whenever the chief emphasis is upon states of feeling, we are observing a nonmissionary religion. What is called emotionalism today is vulnerable at this precise point. We can be glad for the stress upon first-hand religious experience, which was well represented early in the present century, particularly in the wake of Williams James's Gifford Lectures, *The Varieties of Religious Experience*. But we can see now that this stress tended to leave out the missionary emphasis of Basic Christianity. Even in its very best periods, Catholic mysticism showed chiefly a concern for the sanctification of the individual, since mystics do not, for the most part, produce missions. There is, of course, something noble about any life wholly surrendered to God, or that is engaged in the attainment of private sainthood, but, in spite of this, there is always the lurking fallacy of subjectivism. The serious danger of all emphasis upon the inner life, if that is the end of the emphasis, is that of a high level self-centeredness. We are right to cringe when we hear people say that we must begin by loving ourselves. Though we cannot, of course, give what we do not have, if we start by thinking first of ourselves, we miss the point of Christ's teaching and draw a false conclusion from the Golden Rule. Christ's central paradox is that we must begin, not by loving ourselves, but by losing ourselves. Religious experience turns sour if it stands alone, and the man who worships only the God within ends by worshiping himself.

In the long run, the greatest harm to vital religion can come from the inside rather than from avowed enemies. The contemporary emotional wave represented by the renewal of the phenomenon of speaking in tongues may not, finally, be good news. While there is no doubt of the sincerity and the goodwill of those who encourage emotional expressions, they may actually be very far from the fullness of Christ. What they chiefly lack is the outgoing spirit. They miss the combination of service to the brethren and concern for the total welfare of people anywhere which the missionary movement has been able, in spite of mistakes, to demonstrate. Christians are always on the wrong track when they think the injunction is "feel," rather than "go." The hardheaded judgment of the Apostle Paul is the one which Christians need to heed today: "He who speaks in a tongue edifies himself" (I Cor. 14:4). The Apostle's central interest lies never, we must remember, in self-edification, however personally satisfying that may be, but in the word which "speaks to men for their upbuilding and encouragement and consolation" (I Cor. 14:3).

As we look over the human scene we observe that the differences in opportunity are immense. A few of us in Europe and those parts of the globe most influenced by Europeans have almost everything at our command that we could wish. We are within easy reach of excellent medical attention, we have abundant opportunities for education, we are surrounded by books, and we have machines which eliminate a vast amount of routine labor. Of course we have our own forms of misery, but when we compare our lot with the lot of the so-called backward peoples or even our own neighbors we are really amazed at the contrast.

There are large areas which have almost none of the things which make our lives rich and interesting and, in addition, we have even spoiled the system of life these other peoples once had. We have drained off their wealth to make our vaunted progress possible and, in so doing, have given the backward peoples diseases which they did not have before.

Considerations like those mentioned above make it clear that a really spiritual religion is at once a *social* religion and a *missionary* religion. If we *care* about the souls of men, especially when these men are less favored than ourselves, we cannot sit idly by while they are denied those things which would make their lives finer and which we could provide. Indeed, if we admit that part of the evil condition of others is the price that has been paid for the things we enjoy, we are not benevolent when we work for them, but are merely paying a debt long overdue. If a missionary goes to other peoples with a patronizing and condescending air, if he goes to tell them that the things they prize are necessarily worse than the things we prize, he is not looking on human souls with the reverence and wonder which spiritual religion demands. The truly spiritual missionary goes out, not primarily in the interest of a system of teaching, but in the interest of men. He cares for persons; he is wounded in his own spirit when they are denied those things which will develop their sacred and latent powers. He is not so much trying to save them from hell as to save them in the absolute sense discussed in an earlier chapter. He finds men everywhere who are unsaved, i.e., *wasted,* and he cannot accept this situation without action on this part.

The solution of the missionary problem, as is true of so many other problems, lies in the attitude of "not less but more." There is a type of missionary activity which spiritual religion is bound to oppose, but we oppose it best by adopting a larger and more inclusive point of view which makes missionary work as wide as the world. It is a great mistake to divide the world into our lands and the mission field, but the remedy does not lie in giving up the missionary concept; the remedy lies in so enlarging the mission field that it includes our own land as well as others.

If we could make the world our field and if every profession could be undertaken in a missionary spirit, a new day would dawn for mankind. We can see grave evils at home as well as abroad, and we must attack all evils which in any way hinder the growth and development of the Divine Seed. If a missionary is one who nourishes the Seed in others, we need missionaries everywhere, and there is no more noble profession. This might take on many forms, such as medicine or politics or business, but all tasks would be equally noble providing they express human brotherhood and help in some way or other, no matter how small or great, to break down the barriers which keep men back from the growth in life of which they are capable and to which they are divinely called. A nonmissionary Christian is a contradiction of terms. Just as Christianity, rightly understood, entails the abolition of the laity, it also entails the abolition of the nonmissionary class. It is obvious that what has just been said of missionary work applies equally to "social service." Here, also, we must so enlarge the area that the field of endeavor becomes one.

Wherein does the validity of the Christian Movement rest? If it is dependent upon social service, it may be convincing for awhile, but it is not likely to be permanently so. Though missions can be honored for their far-flung work in the establishment of hospitals and schools, all of these may eventually be taken over and operated by governments. Indeed, much of this shift is already occurring in our own time. It is conceivable that someday governments will become sufficiently socialist to accept responsibility for every social need. It is even conceivable that a level of affluence can someday be achieved which will eliminate the necessity of caring for the poor. If, in the long future, these changes occur, the magnificent and compassionate social service performed in thousands of mission stations throughout the world will have historical interest but no more. Will the case for the existence of the World Christian Mission then be stripped of its validity? It will, unless there is another factor which involves real permanence. The conviction that there is a factor has been the inspiration for this book.

The ultimate and permanent case for the Christian Mission rests directly upon the conception that the Christian faith is true. This is the one point which the critics of the enterprise do not touch, except by such an undermining of truth as undermines even their own criticism. In the long run, the best reason for dedication to the spread of the faith of Christ is the conviction that this faith conforms to reality as does no other alternative of which we are aware. Such a position is bound, in our age of supposed tolerance and religious pluralism, to be widely unpopular, but there is not a sufficient reason for rejecting it. It is required to find a *modus.vivendi* according to which, while we seek to be tender with persons, we face resolutely all questions of truth and falsity, insofar as we are able to confront them. If Christianity is not true, there is certainly no adequate reason to reach people with its message, whether they live in China or in California. All of the service tasks can finally be handled in other ways, but the central message of Christ can be handled in only one way, i.e., by committed ambassadors. If the message is not true, the Mission will die and really ought to die; it cannot be maintained permanently by auxiliary enterprises.

The missionary program of the Church of Christ is not simply one aspect of the Christian Cause. It is, instead, the concept which is capable of bringing order and meaning into the entire Christian enterprise. The missionary idea becomes powerful to the extent that it becomes universal in the recognition that the vocation of ministry is really identical with the Christian vocation itself. Because a missionary is defined as one who is "sent," there is a strong tendency to think of the word as denoting only a small number who are officially appointed and consequently supported by their fellow Christians. If, however, we understand that Christ is the Sender, we have a means of overcoming this unfortunate fragmentation. We are then prepared to enunciate and to implement the revolutionary idea of the "Universal Apostolate." When they are loyal to the basic conception, Christians do not merely *send* missionaries; they *are* missionaries. The noblest conception of the true Church is that of a band of people who are engaged in ordinary life and who are conscious of their missionary vocation. The Church, in essence, is a missionary society!

Everyone who reads these words will realize, of course, that the churches which he knows do not fully demonstrate this pattern. Indeed, to some who call themselves members, the idea will seem unrealistic or even bizarre. In actual practice we are so far from demonstrating this pattern that the idea of the Universal Apostolate is not even considered, in many instances, to be a live option. In actuality we think that we are doing very well if we collect a few thousand dollars in one congregation and send it to a national mission board to be administered. No Christian will despise even this kind of giving, because impersonal as it necessarily becomes, it supports far-flung efforts which otherwise could not be continued. But, helpful as such support may be, it is important that we should never permit it to provide us with easy consciences.

However unrealized the idea of a missionary vocation for all committed Christians may be, the promulgation of this dream is far from a wasted effort. In all fields it is valuable to hold aloft ideas of genuine magnitude because, even though they do not achieve full embodiment, the presentation of the standard keeps us dissatisfied and prods us forward at least part way to the goal. This is why we can truly say that the standard is our most precious possession. While we do not, of course, achieve the standard, without it our spiritual poverty would be far worse than it is. Some people speak scornfully of the words "with liberty and justice for all," which Americans repeat in salute to the flag, because these noble conceptions are never fully achieved. Of course they are not, for we are dealing with human ineptitude and greed, but it does not follow from the fact of partial failure that the ideal should not be reaffirmed.

The Universal Apostolate of mothers and doctors and farmers and businessmen has an inherent attractiveness. It is possible that our time may become one of the flowering periods of the Christian Cause, but whether it will or not depends in large measure on the acceptance of the Idea of Mission as both universal and regulative. If this is seriously attempted, it can revolutionize the entire undertaking. Herein lies the hope of a new Reformation!

The Mission of the Church is by the committed to the uncommitted, wherever they may be. This is the chief reason why mere Sunday religion will not suffice. Part of the contemporary stirring in Christian circles today is recognition of the need of going to people where they are. Why should not the Gospel relate to the communities where men and women work, and not merely to those where they sleep?

It is extremely fortunate for the Christian Cause that it is not necessary to try to get its missionaries into the world, since that is where they already are. Christ's ambassadors are already in the Teamsters Union and in the House of Representatives and on the automobile production line. The placing of potential Christian missionaries is so fortunate that it is almost fantastic. If the Church were limited to a shrinking number of professionals, there might be reason for discouragement, but there is immense hope in the scattering of committed Christians as they pursue their secular occupations. The practical task is to make them see the potential of their vocation and to try to help them to be prepared to fulfill it.

More and more the World Mission is now being described in other than geographical or even historical terms. It is not satisfactory to speak of missions as "foreign" and "home," and there is a subtle snobbery in referring to "older" and "younger" churches. By contrast, new and meaningful classifications of the total Mission may profitably be stated in terms of employment. There can be one kind of effort in industry, another in the universities, another in government, and so forth. In the striking phrase of Matthew 13:38, "the field is the world," but, in practice, each person must find his own way in which to participate in the total field.

Hope of renewal of respect for the Mission is justified by isolated signs; the bones may seem to be dried, but they are far from lifeless. It is rational to believe that the miracle of renewal, which has occurred before, can occur again, but the popular criticism which is strong in some areas, though not in all, will grow in effectiveness if it is not answered in a reasonable fashion and answered soon. That is why the most important crisis in the Christian Mission is not financial, but intellectual. Those who believe in the Mission have many tasks, but their first task is to think! If they do this, a true renaissance is possible, but if they do not, the erosion, which is already evident, will proceed unchecked until what has been a remarkable success may end in dismal failure.

The message which it seems foolish to preach, but which,

in reality, changes thousands of lives, is the message of Jesus Christ. The missionary need not defend Western civilization or democracy or natural science or modern technology, though all of these include great merits as well as obvious dangers. He need not defend any ecclesiastical hierarchy or any particular form of church government, even though he recognizes that a person cannot be a Christian alone. The truth which the missionary proclaims, if he understands his vocation, is that God really is, and that He is like Christ. Being like Christ, the One who is Lord of all, including all nations, races, and all cultures, cares for every individual and has made every human being in His own image. The consequent brotherhood stems from the divine paternity as it stems from nothing else in all the world. The effective Christian missionary anywhere is one who tells this story and tells it with all the persuasiveness which he can muster. The Christian missionary is thus synonymous with a Christian, for one who is not a missionary is not a Christian at all.

One of the most revealing results of my effort to understand the phenomenon of the Christian Mission came as I sat with an African man and shared tea in his house. I noted that, though the floor was made of mixed earth and cow dung, which was well packed, the walls of the house were made of bricks. My host was enormously proud of his house, standing, as it does, in contrast to the rondavels of most of his East African neighbors. Because the house was made of brick and this was his chief source of pride, I asked him how he happened to have bricks available. "Oh," he said animatedly, "the missionaries taught us!" Then he brought out a faded photograph of the otherwise unknown emissary of Christ who had taught him to burn bricks. It was the same man who had taught him to read. I realized vividly how mistaken are those people who know of the evangelistic efforts of the missionaries, but know nothing else. The proud owner of the house produces better corn than is normally seen, as well as better coffee trees, and this he attributes to the influence of the agricultural mission. I realized suddenly, in an almost overwhelming fashion, that my host had experienced, in his own lifetime, one of the greatest enlargements that has even been known in a short period, and that nearly all of it was possible because a few men and woman had left their comfortable homes in order to work with unknown people ten thousand miles away.

What is the missionary's right relation to those who have not yet been led to accept Christ as the Center of Certitude? He will have to avoid two contrasting errors, the error of permissiveness and the error of denunciation. The remaining road is admittedly narrow, and the gutters on both sides are wide, but this is the road which Christians are called to travel. On the one hand, we get nowhere at all if we repeat sentimentally the cliché about all roads pointing equally to the top. There is, as Scripture affirms, only one way by which men may be brought to the Father (John 14:6), and if we abandon this, we have little ground left on which to stand . . .

But what about the people who have not explicitly accepted Christ in this life? Are we bound to claim that there is no hope for them? By no means. For one thing, we are not the ones to judge, but, more importantly, we dare not limit God's power. It is undoubtedly true that Christ has been able to reach men and that He continues to reach them, even when they have never heard His name. Early Christians took care of this problem by means of the Logos doctrine, refusing to limit the power of Christ by their own conceptions. He can find men who, at least for awhile, do not know that they are found. Because Christ's light can reach every man (John 1:9), the power of God to draw men to the one true Way is limitless.

It is not the missionary's task to pronounce all other religions and philosophies totally false, for they are not. There are great truths pronounced by nontheistic humanists, as there are valuable insights taught by Buddhists. In humility, the Christian must accept truth wherever it is to be found. What the Christian maintains, however, and what he is able to defend with cogency, is the conviction that whatever is true in all religion is genuinely consummated in Christ. "I am not come to destroy," He said, "but to fulfil" (Matt. 5:17, A.V.). About these words there is an amazing finality.

There is, we conclude, abundant reason to believe that the central convictions of Christianity are true and that the central commitment is justified. What follows them? Simply this: the saving truth must be brought to as many people as possible, regardless of where they live. The case for *foreign* missions, as against work at home, is simply the observation that geographical limitations do not count at all. Differences of geography and differences of culture are not excuses for failure to spread what men and women everywhere deeply need. Herein lies the cogency of the Great Commission.

Selections in Chapter Eight are taken from:
  The Yoke of Christ
  The Validity of the Christian Mission
  The Essence of Spiritual Religion

Chapter Nine

THE IMPORTANCE
OF HUMOR

T he importance of humor has long been a "Trueblood Topic." Many Christians view their world from a humorless position, a perspective which Elton Trueblood strongly challenges. With an emphasis upon the humor that Christ used in his teaching ministry, and with the concern for keeping a balanced disposition between the humorous and the serious sides of life, this chapter helps the reader to recover an important aspect of the Christian faith.

J.R.N.

Solemnity in professions is highly vulnerable. That is why there is so much about pretentious physicians in French comedy. While tragedy deals primarily with the individual, says Bergson, comedy finds its opportunity in classes and groups. All of the ancient Quaker jokes, which are so numerous and, on the whole, so truly funny, turn on the inherent inconsistency which is demonstrated by a crack in the supposed armor of external righteousness. The eighteenth-century Quaker, with his plain garb and his "Thee" and "Thou," was especially vulnerable, as Dr. Johnson detected in one of his famous sallies, preserved for us by Mrs. Piozzi. "Sir," he said, "a man who cannot get to heaven in a green coat, will not find his way thither sooner in a gray one."

Why is some paradox funny and some not? We may as well realize that this is an unanswered question and one which is not likely to receive an adequate answer. We know a little. We know that a paradox is more likely to arouse laughter if it exposes presumption or cuts down to size those who take themselves overseriously. We know that a paradox is more humorous if it does not involve real tragedy or unmerited suffering. We know that it is easier to laugh if the situation presented in the joke is slightly remote in time or in place or in condition. We laugh at the cartoon showing two men in prison with one saying, "There is no place for the little man in crime anymore," partly because most of us are not behind bars.

Far from laughter being incompatible with anguish, it is often the natural expression of deep pain. Coleridge faced this clearly when he tried to see why Hamlet jests when his companions overtake him. "Terror," he says, "is closely connected with the ludicrous; the latter is the common mode by which the mind tries to emancipate itself from terror. The laugh is rendered by nature itself the language of extremes, even as tears are." It is not possible to have genuine humor or true wit without an extremely sound mind, which is always mind capable of high seriousness and a sense of the tragic. This is obviously part of the meaning of Socrates when, after a full night of discussion with Agathon and his other friends, including even Alcibiades, he ended the symposium, at daybreak, by insisting that anyone who can write tragedy can also write comedy, because the fundamental craft is the same in each of them. Kierkegaard echoed this conclusion when he said that the comic and the tragic touch each other at the absolute point of infinity.

What is really new is the dominance of an angry mood. Those who are personally angry and who try to whip up anger in others, particularly in the marching mob, tend to lose all perspective. The mood, of course, is enhanced as it is expressed, and most of all, if it is expressed by a group in which the vociferous judgments are mutually reinforcing.

An extremely disturbing factor in the popular moralizing is that it is as unlaughing as it is unloving. There seems to be little opportunity for humor when people are perpetually angry. It is important to note that even the supposedly humorous magazines are now less productive of laughter as they engage, even more deeply, in moral crusading and in violent denunciation of those with whom they happen to disagree.

The emergence of the mood of unlaughing concern has appeared, not among the oppressed, but among the affluent and the overprivileged. It is among these, rather than among the poor, that there is evidence of the most extreme self-righteousness. Partly out of a sense of guilt for having been the recipients of too much, these crusaders go forth with the utmost grimness to denounce the social order by which they are supported.

One mistake that we have made in our Christian social witness is that we have been too uniformly serious. When we are disappointed with our fellow men and with ourselves, as we inevitably are, laughter is a solvent. It helps us greatly to know that Christ laughed, and to sense the variety of His humor. Some of His teachings, which are completely mystifying on the assumption that He was deadly serious, suddenly become clear if it is recognized that He was joking. Part of the trouble with our standard protest marches and sit-ins is not that they are lacking in moral emphasis, but that they are, in one sense, too moral. Always there is some claim about injustice of unfairness; always there is unqualified condemnation of the opposition; always there is dead seriousness. We need to remember that it is possible to exhibit an inverted Puritanism, and that the extreme concern for morals is the essence of fanaticism. It is highly pertinent to our own situation to know that some of the best of Christ's humor refers to the predicament of the unlaughing Pharisee. The claimant to self-righteousness is always a bit ridiculous, but he could be saved from the worst excesses if he could stop and laugh heartily. The recovery of laughter would be more than a relief; it would be a genuine social service.

The widespread failure to recognize and to appreciate the humor of Christ is one of the most amazing aspects of the era named for Him. Anyone who reads the Synoptic Gospels with a relative freedom from presuppositions might be expected to see that Christ laughed, and that He expected others to laugh, but our capacity to miss this aspect of His life is phenomenal. We are so sure that He was always deadly serious that we often twist His words in order to try to make them conform to our preconceived mold. A misguided piety has made us fear that acceptance of His obvious wit and humor would somehow be mildly blasphemous or sacrilegious. Religion, we think, is serious business, and serious business is incompatible with banter.

It is true that our common lives are helped by both genuine religion and genuine humor. In the teaching of Christ the two forms are conjoined.

Full recognition of Christ's humor has been surprisingly rare. In many of the standard efforts to write the Life of Christ there is no mention of humor at all, and when there is any, it is usually confined to a hint or two. Frequently, there is not one suggestion that He ever spoke other than seriously. It is to Renan's credit that he sensed the existence of the humorous element in the Gospels and called it striking, though he did not develop his insight in detail. Tennyson, in pointing out the paradox that humor is generally most fruitful in the most solemn spirits, said, "You will even find it in the Gospel of Christ."

The recognition that Christ understood and demonstrated humor helps us to see a greater profundity in the dictum that it is impossible to enter the Kingdom except as we become little children (Mark 10:15). The child laughs because he has not yet been brainwashed and thereby blinded to the truly amusing. The serious Dane understood the connection between childlikeness and humor, and thereby gave us a new understanding of how the becoming as a little child is one of the necessary conditions of entrance into the Kingdom. "The humorous effect," he wrote in *Concluding Unscientific Postscript*, "is produced by letting the childlike trait reflect itself in the consciousness of totality." The normal child laughs a great deal, partly because his mind is not yet accustomed to the surprising paradoxes of reality. The humorist is one who is still partly a child in that he "possesses the childlike quality, but is not possessed by it." He sees the grotesque as grotesque because, by God's grace, he has been saved from the sad fate of taking it for granted. It is part of the greatness of Kierkegaard that he understood the theory of the significance of the childlike; it is part of the greatness of Jesus Christ that he *demonstrated* it.

Of all the mistakes which we make in regard to the humor of Christ, perhaps the worst mistake is our failure, or our unwillingness, to recognize that Christ used deliberately preposterous statements to get His point across. When we take a deliberately preposterous statement and, from a false sense of piety, try to force some literal truth out of it, the result is often grotesque. The playful, when interpreted with humorless seriousness, becomes merely ridiculous. An excellent illustration of this is a frequent handling of the gigantic dictum about the rich man and the needle's eye, an elaborate figure which appears in identical form in all three of the Synoptics. "It is easier," said Jesus, "for a camel to go through the eye of a needle than for a rich man to enter the kingdom of God" (Mark 10:25). This categorical statement, given with no qualifications whatever, follows, in all three accounts, the story of a wealthy man who came to Jesus to ask seriously how he might have eternal life. He claimed to have kept the standard commandments, but he went away sorrowfully when told that, at least in his case, it would be necessary to divest himself of all of his possessions.

We are informed that Christ's hearers were greatly astonished, and well they might have been, if they took the dictum literally, as they apparently did. Taken literally, of course, the necessary conclusion is that no one who is not in absolute poverty can enter the Kingdom, because most people have some riches, and it is impossible for a body as large as that of a camel, hump and all, to go through an aperture as small as the eye of a needle. For humorous purposes this is evidently the same camel swallowed by the Pharisee when he carefully rejected the gnat. That the listeners failed to see the epigram about the needle's eye as a violent metaphor is shown by their question, "Then who can be saved?" (Mark 10:26).

By making the statement in such an exaggerated form, termed by Chesterton the *giantesque,* Christ made sure that it was memorable, whereas a prosy, qualified statement would certainly have been forgotten. The device is mirrored in our conventional Texas story, which no one believes literally, but which everyone remembers. Christ made his point, so that millions remember it today, though the first hearers misunderstood and kept it accurately only because it was so bizarre.

We need not be astonished if the fisherman failed to see Christ's humor about the needle's eye, but it is truly shocking to find that many contemporary Christians continue to make the same mistake, yet make it in a more elaborate way. Because they cannot bear the bold figure of the patently impossible, they say that Jesus did not really mean by the eye of a needle that through which people put thread for sewing. He meant, they say, a gate in Jerusalem which was so low that a camel could wriggle through it only with extreme difficulty, and even then without his load, which had to be removed if the passage was to be accomplished. Thus, many moderns believe, they save the words of Christ from appearing preposterous. What they miss, by this devious explanation, in contradistinction to the plain sense, is that there is good reason to suppose that Christ *meant* His words to sound preposterous. We spoil the figure, and lose all the robustness, when we tone it down. Christ had a revolutionary message to give and He knew that He could not make Himself understood by speaking mildly. He said that, following John, "the good news of the kingdom of God is preached, and every one enters it violently" (Luke 16:16). We do not know all that He meant by "violently," but we do know that there was an element of "violence" in His speech, a feature which comes through to us today even after the toning down on the part of the reporters.

The humor of Christ does not employ all of the humorous forms known, though it employs many which are familiar to us in subsequent literature. Perhaps the chief difference between Christ's humor and ours today is revealed in the fact that, in our ordinary experience, we make abundant use of the humorous anecdote, for its own sake. The laugh for which we strive is often the sole justification of the entire effort. We seek humor for humor's sake. There seems to be little or none of this in the recorded words of Christ, where the purpose is always the revelation of some facet of truth which would not otherwise be revealed. The humor of Christ is employed, it would appear, only because it is a means of calling attention to what would, without it, remain hidden or unappreciated. Truth, and truth alone, is the end.

That a gentle use of irony came early in Christ's public career is shown by His appeal to the very first of those who were willing to commit themselves to Him, and to His cause. These were two fishermen, Simon and Andrew, and to His cause. These were two fishermen, Simon and Andrew, and He reached these first recruits by a witty reference to their occupation. It is hard to think that they did not smile when He said, "Follow me, and I will make you fishers of men" (Mark 1:17). The term "fishers of men" has, of course, become so much a part of our total language that it is not striking to us, but once it must have been. The irony is so slight that it could never produce a boisterous laugh, but it could elicit a smile.

Much more striking as an example of Christ's irony, is the application of a nickname to one of these men, Simon (Matt. 16:18). Peter got his nickname when, in the district of Caesarea Philippi, he achieved, suddenly, the tremendous insight concerning who his Leader was. Even on this solemn occasion Christ proved that He could joke and He did so by giving Simon the fisherman the most improbable of nicknames. In our terminology, He called the fellow "Rocky" and the name stuck. The paradox is obvious, for

Simon was anything but stable and durable, which is what rocky things are supposed to be. No sooner did Simon receive his nickname, Peter, than he rejected his Master's teaching and rebuked him, whereupon Christ said to him, with sudden fierceness, "Get behind me, Satan! You are a hindrance to me; for you are not on the side of God, but of men" (Matt. 16:23). That Peter was unstable was proved by his showing himself to be both a liar and a coward at the time of the trial before the high priest. Peter "followed at a distance" and sat in the courtyard, but when he was asked whether he was one of Christ's companions, he answered, "I do not know what you mean" (Matt. 26:71), and later said, "I do not know the man."

If this was the "Rock" on which the redemptive fellowship had to be built, it certainly seemed to be a shaky foundation. The house was obviously being built on sand, at best, and how, from such an infirm base, would it be possible to penetrate the very gates of hell? Here is paradox on paradox, yet it was more than a joke, though it *was* a joke. Jesus saw more in Simon and the other inadequate men than met the eye. The humorous nickname "Rocky" was a prediction of future stability, even though, at the time, it was patently absurd. At the moment, it must have seemed like our practice of calling the fat man "Slim" and the tall man "Shorty." But it was more than that. The very irony served a redemptive purpose, in that the power of expectancy was demonstrated in the revolutionary result. We do not know much about Peter's personal life, or about his wife, or even, apart from mere tradition, how he reached his end, but we do know that he preached the resurrection with persuasive power, that he recognized the necessity of liberation of all Christians from the bondage of the Hebrew law, and that he was a tower of strength in the infant church. The joke ceased to be merely a joke, because what began as shifting rubble was transformed, by the influence of the Living Christ, into solid rock. Peter he was not; but Peter he became! What started as a joke ended as fact.

The dividing line which separates irony and sarcasm is sometimes a narrow one and is easily crossed. Truth compels us to say that it is sometimes crossed in the words recorded in the Gospels. In a few instances the irony becomes so exaggerated that it is really sarcastic. We do well to note carefully the instances of this, inasmuch as Christ must have felt that the gravity of some problems required a sterner treatment.

An excellent illustration is that about the keeping of the law. In Luke's account we read, "It is easier for heaven and earth to pass away, than for one dot of the law to become void" (Luke 16:17). The upholders of the law, committed to its very minutiae, were more concerned with it than with the whole of heaven and earth. The Pharisees could see the whole universe destroyed with more equanimity than they were able to muster if they witnessed hungry men rubbing out heads of wheat on the Sabbath or if they saw a man healed at a time when healing was ceremonially forbidden. Now the clear point is that Christ valued the world more than every jot and tittle of the law or even more than the entire law. We know this from the record of His own practice and from His emphasis upon mercy rather than upon sacrifice. If the Sabbath was made for man, rather than man for the Sabbath, then something in earth and heaven was more valuable than the law, including its most trivial details. The word "dot" is obviously meant to signify a trivial detail. These details were intimately connected with the ceremonial rules of the Temple, but Christ said boldly, "I tell you, something greater than the temple is here" (Matt. 12:6).

There is no evidence that the reporters of the pungent saying about its being easier to lose the world than to lose a detail of the law understood it as a joke at all. Very likely they missed the sarcasm, as some of us have done more recently. The seriousness with which the remark was received is indicated by the form which it is given in Matthew. "For truly, I say to you, till heaven and earth pass away, not an iota, not a dot, will pass from the law until all is accomplished." If this was sober truth, then we cannot avoid the conclusion and the early Christians who ceased to require circumcision and who rejected dietary laws were wholly wrong! If what Christ said was sober prose it was simply false! The only alternative solution is that He was joking. His words make sense only if they are exaggerated banter.

Why we miss so much of this, even today, requires some rational explanation. Why, for instance, do we miss the sarcasm about courts of law which appears in both Matthew and Luke? Whatever else we can say about Christ's teaching, the main tenor of it was not that of prudence or of compromise. Indeed, we are told that the deepest things are hidden from the wise and prudent, i.e., the people who know how to look out for number one (Matt. 11:25). But what are we to make of this counsel of prudence?

> "As you go with your accuser before the magistrate, make an effort to settle with him on the way, lest he drag you to the judge, and the judge hand you over to the officer, and the officer put you in prison. I tell you, you will never get out till you have paid the very last copper" (Luke 12:58, 59).

Because we are so familiar with these words, we fail to see how shocking they are. Because we are so bemused by the desire to make them creditable, we twist them into a preconceived pattern. But what do the words really say? Here is a picture of the clear miscarriage of justice which must have been all too familiar to Christ's original hearers. The rude fishermen might miss some of the finer points of irony, but they could hardly miss the sarcasm about justice. They knew what it was to have the last copper exacted, even though the offense was minor or even though the charge was unjust.

What Christ seems to be advocating is a clever deal or a bribe. Pay off your accuser or fix it up with him somehow, regardless of justice! Translated into our language, "It may prove to be cheaper to pay the officer than to pay the court, so why not try?" Perhaps that would be the path of wisdom in a world where leading men "bind heavy burdens, hard to bear, and lay them on men's shoulders; but they themselves will not move them with their finger" (Matt. 23:4). If this be humor, it is humor with an acid touch. The account of going before the judges is so vivid that it sounds like the voice of experience. It is not unreasonable to suppose that Christ had already been in their clutches. But that the prudential advice is sarcastic is indicated by the fact that it is preceded immediately by a vivid query completely at variance with the acceptance of mere prudential advice: "And why do you not judge for yourselves what is right?" (Luke 12:57). Here is the antithesis of supine accomodation to unjust treatment. And then the point is driven home, for those willing and able to see it, by a lampoon.

Though the battle of Christ had to be waged on two fronts, one of these occupied far more time and effort than did the other. This was the front against the religious opposition, represented primarily by the enmity of the Pharisees. Here the strategy of laughter was more appropriate and effective than on the political front, for bigotry is peculiarly vulnerable to ridicule. It is surprising to some, though it ought not to be, that Christ's most intractable enemies were those who saw, in Him and His teaching, a threat to their own religious program. While the Roman power, vested in the procurator, must be held accountable for His actual execution, the truth is that the procurator acted reluctantly, and that the development would not have moved to its tragic end had it not been for the fierce enmity engendered in the members of the Sanhedrin. Religious enemies are the fiercest that there are! Because we really know this, we give full assent to Pascal's famous epigram, "Men never do evil so completely and cheerfully as when they do it from religious conviction."

The consequences of Christ's rejection of the dismal are great, not only for common life, but also for theology. If Christ laughed a great deal, as the evidence shows, and if He is what He claimed to be, we cannot avoid the logical conclusion that there is laughter and gaiety in the heart of God. The deepest conviction of all Christian theology is the affirmation that the God of all the world is like Jesus Christ. Because the logical development is from the relatively known to the relatively unknown, the procedure is not from God to Christ, but from Christ to God. If we take this seriously we conclude that God cannot be cruel, or self-centered or vindictive, or even lacking in humor.

Selections in Chapter Nine are taken from:
The Humor of Christ
The Life We Prize
The New Man for Our Time

Chapter
Ten

THE CHURCH
OF THE FUTURE

Does the church have a future? Elton Trueblood strongly believes that it does, but if the church of the future is to be a potent, dynamic influence, certain changes of emphasis must be made. In this, the final chapter of this anthology, the pen of Dr. Trueblood leads Christians to a clear understanding of their purpose, and then shares how this purpose can be realized in the church that is yet to be.

J.R.N.

The worst nightmare is not the disappearance of Christianity, but its continued existence on a low level. This is what may occur, for a while, unless a more demanding rationality emerges in the Church of Christ. The story of Christian history includes, we must admit, frequent decline, as well as advance. Because there is no known insurance against loss of devotion, this may occur even to the contemporary bands, but the good news is that, when old Christian societies die, others can arise to accept the responsibility of attack upon the world. This is how the Church of Christ operates.

The Christian faith may, indeed, survive in the future as it has in the past, but does this mean that the Church will also survive? It is at this point that the questions of so many thoughtful people are becoming insistent. Is the Church really needed in the new age which we are entering? Underlying this honest doubt is the more or less explicit conviction that a churchless Christianity is a practical possibility. Unless we deal seriously with this widespread conviction we are not likely to be able to reach contemporary minds.

It is not difficult to see why the dream of a churchless Christianity is currently fashionable. Keep Christ, many suggest, but set Him free from all of the ecclesiastical trappings which have accumulated during the years that have intervened since He lived on earth. Why not return to the simple teachings of the Galilean, eliminating all boards and commissions and fund drives? Isn't there a real danger that the love of Christ may be forgotten in the multitude of conferences, synods, assemblies, and councils? Why not settle for individual love and kindness, without the bother of regular worship, sacraments, and preaching? Because many have noted that the strongest opposition which Christ met on earth was that of the religious establishment, they are bound to wonder whether the same situation does not face Him again today. Perhaps the Church is superfluous, even to Christ Himself.

Part of the doubt about both the efficacy and the necessity of the Church arises from the observed fact that, in numerous areas, congregations are already withering. Consider, for example, the beautiful meetinghouses of New England. It is delightful to any lover of architecture to study the photographs of these wonderful buildings, the white spire in the village being able to lift almost anyone. It is a distinct shock, however, to realize that a good many of these buildings are now used only once a year. Some are not the scenes of gathered fellowships of local residents week after week, and could not even be maintained apart from the efforts of historical societies and local associations formed for the purpose of keeping the physical structures intact. Though we are glad that there are such associations, we are well aware that they are certainly not the Church. However pathetic an unused building may be, regular congregations which include practically no young people are almost equally pathetic. It is actually possible to point to congregations which include nobody under the age of sixty. Most church buildings, moreover, are far larger than any present need would justify. Is it strange, then, that the idea of a churchless Christianity should be considered as a live option?

That the idea of a churchless Christianity is not intrinsically absurd is evident when we realize that, in most of the world's religions, there has never been anything identical with what we mean by the Church. It is wholly possible to have shrines and priestly orders and scriptures and ceremonies without the existence of gathered communities of ordinary men and women whose faith is nurtured by a living fellowship. Even orders of monks and nuns can exist without the concurrent existence of gathered churches.

Unless we pay close attention to the historical evidence, we are strongly tempted to forget the essential uniqueness of the Christian Church as an expression of the religious life. Indeed, it is a bit shocking to note that the ancient Greeks and Romans who were, in some ways, highly religious, possessed nothing even similar to what we mean by a church. The beautiful temples which we admire, even in ruins, had little or no relation to the kind of experience which we take for granted, with its regularity of group worship, its Sunday School instruction, its suppers, its youth fellowships, its choirs, etc. The leaders of the classic civilization had shrines, priests, and occasional festivals, but all of these together fall short of what we mean by a gathered group of followers of Christ who, though they live and work in the ordinary world, are members one of another.

What we need desperately to understand is that, though it is conceivable that the Christian faith may go on without the organized Church, such an event, if such should occur, would involve a radical alteration in the character of the entire Christian Movement. Because of its realistic estimate of man, Christianity has always seen the necessity of the Church if vitality is to be maintained. Angels might not need the supports and the reminders which the Church provides, but men, as we know very well, are not angels and not likely to become such.

The only reasonable conclusion is that all of the arguments for the probability of the continuance of the faith also turn out to be arguments for the continuance of the *Church*, since the two cannot logically be separated. Individual Christianity is a self-contradiction! Unless there is a sense of "one another" there is no sense of the Living Christ. Though the Church, as we observe it, frequently fills us with frustrations, we know, if we are realists, that it provides the only way in which Christians can be faithful to their Lord. Nothing was accomplished by individual voices crying in the wilderness, but the early fellowship, fallible as it was, produced even the New Testament. It was because of *congregations* that there was a demand for the writing of the Gospels! Furthermore, most of the Epistles have no meaning except in reference to the fellowships to which they are addressed, and even the last book of the Bible begins with letters to seven existing congregations.

The more we ponder, the more we are likely to conclude that the Church will have a future. The Church, of course, may change greatly in its human structure, but the probability is that it will become more important rather than less so. It must become more important because the need for a redemptive fellowship will be increasingly urgent. If men are honest they will recognize the occasional need to be alone, but, if they are also intelligent, they will recognize, at the same time, that what they do alone has far more significance if, at some point in their lives, they experience a deep sharing with other unworthy disciples of the same Lord.

Popular criticism of "organized" Christianity demands careful examination. There can be over-organization, but there is nothing intrinsically wrong about being organized. As a matter of fact, organization is necessary for almost any valuable accomplishment. We are helped, in this regard, if we remember that early Christianity was itself highly organized. Witness the superb system of visitation of which we read in the Pauline Epistles and in the Book of Acts. The way in which the Roman Empire was criss-crossed by the little teams is impressive to any reader who is not so familiar with the story that he takes it for granted. The organization included the collection of funds, in some parts, to help those who suffered in distant places. We are the more amazed at the success of this endeavor when we are reminded of the difficulties of travel and of communication. We cannot avoid the conclusion that, if Christianity had not been "organized," it would not have survived.

The question before thoughtful Christians now is not *whether* they will be organized, but *how*. Some inadequate forms and some unproductive fellowships ought clearly to be abandoned. It must never be supposed that there was some perfect form of the Church in the past to which we ought now to return. Indeed, the entire idea of Restoration is one which, the more we analyze it, we are bound to reject as unworthy. Unless we are addicted to primitivism, we see nothing wrong with development. Even Penn's famous phrase "Primitive Christianity Revived," while undoubtedly an effective slogan, was never much more. There is not, in fact, some ideal system of elders and deacons and bishops which once existed and which it is our duty to reproduce. Worship we must experience, but the simple truth is that the entire New Testament does not contain one single order of worship. We can understand a little, from our study of the fourteenth chapter of First Corinthians, of how the early Christians gathered, but we are not furnished with adequate details. Even if we did know how they operated, such knowledge would not produce a norm for our own action today and tomorrow. The Christian faith does not look back to a Golden Age in the past, but always to a more glorious possibility in the future. Whatever the Christians of ancient Corinth did, we should try to improve on their practice, for they were conspicuously imperfect. All of our orientation toward the future is supported by the remarkably hopeful utterance, "I have yet many things to say to you, but you cannot bear them now" (John 16:12).

Few items of the gospel are more moving than the brief sentence, "Something greater than the temple is here" (Matt. 12:6). Much of our endeavor, as we face the future of the Church, is that of trying to understand together what the character of this "something greater" may be. We get some hint of what the "something greater" may have been, in Christ's own dream, when we note where He placed the emphasis. The Church, as He envisioned it, was made up of those who were engaged in a healing task. Because people were harassed and helpless, like sheep without a shepherd, workers were needed, *and these workers were the Church!*

It is a great moment in any life when a Christian comes to realize that the Church, as Christ formed it long ago, was not a crowd watching a performance, but persons engaged in a ministry to other persons. We cannot appreciate all that Christ had in mind when he spoke of the Church, but we have made at least one step in that direction when we see that He was recruiting a society of ministers in daily life. If this vision can be implemented, the future of the Church is no longer doubtful! The conception of Christ as the perpetual Recruiter, and the members of the Church as His team, is one of such intrinsic appeal that it is not dependent upon changing fashions, including fashions of theology. The Church is the enlargement of the "Twelve," and, like the original Twelve, it is bound to include unworthy persons. Part of the miracle is the demonstrated fact that unworthy persons, when ignited by the central fire of Christ, are able to ignite other unworthy persons. After leaving the synagogue at Nazareth, to which He may never have returned, Christ started something really new in religion. The key sentence, which shows the expulsive character of the new fellowship, is as follows: "And he called to him the twelve, and began to send them out" (Mark 6:7). Here was something conspicuously greater than the temple and its ritual. Whereas the temple had been centripetal, the Church was intended to be centrifugal.

Once we are able to understand that emphasis upon the ministry is the key to new vitality, our strategy becomes clear. What we need to do is to draw into the ministry the various groups which, for one reason or another, are now partly excluded from it. The exciting adventure centers largely upon the effort to liberate the potential human forces which are now largely untapped. It is in the employment of wasted powers that there can be the greatest single difference between the Church of today and the Church of tomorrow. The involvement of those who are not now members of Christ's team may produce important changes both in their lives and in the life of the world. We are driven to this when we realize how poor we are and how rich we might be.

Four groups, potentially valuable to the Christian Cause, are, at the present time, relatively untapped human resources. These four are *laymen, women, retired persons,* and *youth.* Some persons in each of these four groups are now involved in the promotion of the Christian Cause, but they represent only a tiny fraction of the power which is currently available. It will require more thinking than we have yet employed to know how to liberate these urgently needed but partially undeveloped human assets. Because failure to make use of what is available is not only sinful, but stupid, we must give careful thought to this fourfold task.

1. *The inclusion of laymen in the ministry* has already been partly accomplished, though much remains to be done. Indeed, the theory and practice of the lay ministry has been the greatest single mark of emerging vitality in the Church of the twentieth century. The crucial date in this emergence, so far as our century is concerned, is 1931. In that year of deep economic depression John R. Mott gave the Ayer Lectures at the Colgate-Rochester Divinity School and started a fundamentally new chapter in the life of the Church. The title of the lectures, and also of the book which was published in 1932, was *Liberating the Lay Forces of Christianity.* Dr. Mott was not, of course, the first to encourage lay religion, but he was able to catch the imagination of Christian people as few before him had done. As Chairman of the International Missionary Council and President of the World Alliance of Young Men's Christian Associations, his words carried great weight, especially among contemporary students.

Much has occurred during the subsequent forty years in the growth of the lay ministry, and numerous voices have been added to Dr. Mott's, but in many ways his appeal was original. What was unique was the conception of liberation. He saw men of wisdom and experience who were largely unused because they were bound by a false idea, the idea that the Christian ministry is the proprietary domain of

clergymen. The very notion that there is a genuine difference between clergy and laity must be recognized as a
heresy, the division between them being the most deadly of
all schisms! Partly because of the pioneering thinking of Dr.
Mott, the conviction that in Christ there is neither lay nor
clerical has become one of the most liberating ideas of the
twentieth century. Not all accept or understand this bold
conception even yet, but a good many, including some
readers of this book, realize that only by faithfulness to it
can we erect something bigger than the temple.

It would be foolish to fail to admit that there is resistance
to lay liberation and that there are numerous congregations
in which no serious start has been made in this redemptive
innovation. There are, indeed, supposedly committed
Christians who see nothing intrinsically absurd about the
expectation that one man should be inspired to speak fifty-
two times a year, while the others are never expected to
have the experience at all. The easy procedure is to go on
with a society in which a few speak and many listen, but
this is the road to death.

It must be frankly admitted that some members actually
prefer the position of noninvolvement. Obviously it is
much less demanding to settle for attendance at some
gatherings, combined with a modest financial support,
than to enter into the ministry. There is nothing really surprising about the fact that so many prefer to delegate their
religious responsibility to an individual who is hired to do
the task, much as they hire a man to make out income tax
returns. People often prefer this because it is less costly, but
in religion the results of such a division of labor are uniformly damaging. Christianity, in spite of its miraculous
history, decays unless a fair proportion of its adherents
accept joyously the conception of the Church of Christ as a
servant society, made up of those who are engaged in the
work of the world at the same time that they are engaged in
being Christ's representatives. Some teachers have been
saying this for a generation, and there have been visible

effects of this teaching, but more must now pursue the theme, because the idea has not taken sufficient hold.

Elevation of the potential ministry of the lay Christian involves no depreciation of the work of the pastor. Indeed, emphasis upon lay ministry, far from making the pastor less important, makes him far more so. "I do not," said Mott in 1931, "share the view that the Christian ministry does not have so important and so necessary a function as in the past." The reason why the idea of the Church, as a society of ministers in common life, requires the pastoral ministry is that the pastor is the one person who is most likely to be able, if he gives his attention to the task, "to build up, to train, to inspire, to direct the lay forces." There is a place for the ministry of persons who are employed full time in factories and shops and government offices, but there is, without contradiction, a place for the ministry of men who are freed from the necessity of secular earning. Someone needs to work at the job of *calling out the latent forces.*

The Church of the future will have pastors for the simple reason that vital lay religion does not emerge unless somebody works at the task of its development. The primary professional ministry of the future will undoubtedly be the ministry of encouragement. What is more exciting than the release of human powers which have long lain dormant? We need genuine professionals, not in the sense that they are skilled in ceremonial performances, but in the far deeper sense that they have learned the skill of drawing out the powers of other men. This is precisely what is meant today by the "equipping" or "enabling" ministry (Eph. 4:12), and it ought to become the center of professional pastoral training in the future. In the Church of the future the liberator of other men's powers will be more, rather than less, important. We may not actually employ the term "liberator" rather than "pastor," but that is what we shall have to mean if there is to be a new chapter in the life of the Church.

It is important to do some new thinking about religious professionalism. This is required as we reexamine our total enterprise, in the willingness to omit anything which does not meet the real needs of men. We soon realize that there is a sense in which religious professionalism is undesirable, and also a sense in which it is necessary. Professionalism is deeply wrong if it inhibits the involvement of the non-professionals. This is often what results when a congregation employs a staff which is too large. There is, of course, the consequent problem of raising money to pay salaries, rather than to feed the hungry, but this is not the primary difficulty. Far worse is the almost inevitable undermining of the unpaid involvement of the ordinary members of what is supposed to be a team. Over and over, when the question is asked why lay members are not active participants in the conduct of public worship, as regular readers of the Scriptures, the standard answer is that associate pastors have been employed and that they have to be used visibly. Whenever staff members perform duties which lay members need to do, this is a sign of sickness rather than of health.

The emphasis upon the liberation of laymen must never make the mistake of denying that there is a significant place for the professional. There is nothing wrong with being a professional writer, with the conscious development of clarity; there is, likewise, nothing wrong with being a professional speaker, using all of the powers of speech to convey the truth and knowing when to stop, as the amateur often does not. We need men who are genuine professionals in listening to others, drawing out of them ideas and hopes, of which they might not have become aware, without intelligent assistance.

2. *Women constitute a second group of Christians whose liberation would add enormously to the power of Christ in the world.* Though, in comparison with other world religions, the Christian record in the involvement of women is relatively good, it is not good enough. Women were Christ's intimate

companions (Luke 8:2); women stood at the cross; women reported the resurrection; and women are mentioned frequently in the New Testament Epistles. In the noble passage in which the term "Yokefellow" appears as a synonym for a practicing Christian recruit, there is reference to two women who, says Paul, "labored side by side with me in the gospel" (Phil. 4:3). Though Paul, at one time in his career, took a dim view of speaking on the part of women (I Cor. 14:34, 35), he advanced to the height of recognizing that sexual distinctions are absolutely meaningless in the service of Christ. This is the clear significance of Galatians 3:28. Because we are "all one in Christ Jesus," it follows logically, Paul saw, that "there is neither male nor female."

In spite of this brave start, women have not been used in the Church exactly as men. In numerous contemporary congregations the women worshipers outnumber the men, sometimes by as much as two to one, but most of the important leadership is still in male hands. We do not need to subscribe to the rhetoric of the Women's Liberation Movement to see that this situation is deeply wrong, and it is especially clear that it is stupid, when the Church is literally fighting, against great odds, for its very life. It is foolish to neglect available power when it is desperately needed. Just as, forty years ago, John R. Mott started us thinking seriously about "liberating the lay forces of Christianity," so now, in our effort to create an intelligent future, we must help one another to think carefully about liberating the female forces. This is how the Christian movement proceeds; one wave of liberation follows another! We must try to see which sector needs major attention at each particular time.

Women are, of course, used in the contemporary Church, but they are not, for the most part, used in the ways where their contribution would add the greatest strength. Women cook congregational suppers; women teach children and other women; women organize missionary societies; women operate social circles; women serve on altar guilds. Having made such a list, we soon realize that we are hard pressed if we try to enlarge it. Where we fail is in the encouragement of Christian women to provide intellectual leadership. That such leadership is possible is proven by reference to the work of Dorothy Sayers, Olive Wyon, Georgia Harkness, and a few more, but it is not possible to extend such a list as we might wish to do.

The possible employment of women's intellectual life provides more concrete hope than can be found almost anywhere. In spite of the increasing fashion of employment of women outside the home, in business and industry, it is still true that women, on the whole, have more free time in their lives than do most men. After the children have departed, there is often a magnificent chance to start a new productive chapter, if only women could have the imagination to see the opportunity. Why are we not intelligent enough to see that the ministry of women is our unexploited asset? There is no doubt about the dedication of women, often surpassing that of men; the doubt is whether we can harness the dedication in more than trivial ways. Most men, however devoted they may be, are too tired at the end of competitive days of labor to engage in creative thinking, but there are thousands of women who do not encounter this handicap to rational inquiry.

We need help at almost every point in the articulation of our faith. This articulation cannot be accomplished except as there emerges an entire generation of Christian intellectuals. These are more likely to come among women than from any other source, but they will not appear unless we produce a mood of expectancy. Women may surpass men in the modern world in setting up book tables to help the members and attenders in the guidance of their reading; women may start serious classes in theology to help distraught and confused people to think clearly about the deepest issues of their lives; women may produce books which will do for their generation what Dorothy Sayers did so magnificently for hers.

Most people, when they speak of the ministry of women,

think at once of women clergy, a conception which some reject. Though we have women preachers, and though Lutherans have now decided, for the first time in their history, to ordain women, the number is small. For example, although women comprise 57.4 percent of the membership of the United Presbyterian Church, they comprise only one half of one percent of the teaching elders and only 15.75 percent of the ruling elders. These figures will undoubtedly change radically in the immediate future, because there is no good reason why women should not speak and counsel precisely as men do, but this is not where the main growth seems to be coming. The main growth is that of the mergence of new ministries which women themselves are able to invent and encourage. One indication of what is expected is the appearance in 1970 of a new book by a Christian woman, who started writing at the Southern Baptist Convention at New Orleans in June, 1969.

Some women, even more than men, may resist the idea of a Christian intellectual vocation for themselves, because they are so keenly aware of their inadequacy. The clear answer to this objection is that people can *grow* and that they are supposed to grow. One woman at The Church of the Saviour in Washington, D.C. was practically illiterate when she was enrolled in Christian study, but before her death she was a resource leader for the pastor, Gordon Cosby, in regard to some details of modern theology. Furthermore, we are helped by remembering the way in which inferior powers may be glorified by proper use. That most of the early Christians felt inadequate is indicated by Paul's specific words. "Few of you," he wrote, "are men of wisdom, by any human standard" (I Cor. 1:26, NEB). One in our century who understood this thoroughly and stated it clearly was John D. Rockefeller, Jr. Speaking in 1916, he said, "In carrying on the world's work, the Lord is not able to select perfect tools that are exactly fitted for each requirement; He has to use such human instruments as are available."

3. *The third major human resource that is essentially un-exploited is that of retired people.* Now that it is standard for those who work both with hand and brain to retire at the age of sixty-five or sooner, we are producing a vast human reservoir waiting to be tapped. We have, of course, given some attention to this phenomenon, especially in the creation of retirement communities, but, for the most part, we have not seen the possibilities so far as the Christian Movement is concerned. Because of better public health, many retired people are physically and mentally strong, with an accumulation of wisdom about life which comes from long experience. It is fundamentally ridiculous to assume that such people should concentrate on playing shuffleboard for twenty years! But what is the alternative?

The most beneficent change in regard to retired people is a change in their own self-image, and this is the point at which the Christian faith can make a genuine contribution. *For the Christian, retirement means liberation for service, and it means nothing else.* The retired Christian physician, if he understands the gospel, asks where people need medical care, but cannot afford it. Liberation from the necessity of earning, which retirement income accomplishes more and more, simply places numerous modest persons in the same category to which John R. Mott belonged all of his mature life. Very early he was "liberated" by a group of men who undertook to pay his bills so that he could give himself to a career of unmercenary service. Because this is an idea which is little understood, and often not even contemplated, it is one in which, by its dissemination, the Church of tomorrow can make a difference. It must be made clear, however, that the opportunity of the retired Christian is not to serve the Church, but the *world*.

4. *Young People constitute not only the greatest challenge to the Church of the future, but also its greatest hope.* The evidence of the probable continuance of the Church in succeeding centuries is valid, but its validity depends on the possibility of attracting a far larger proportion of young people. There

is good reason to believe that this can be done, but it will not be done unless we meet the conditions. One of the conditions is an honest admission of how radically we are failing in gaining the participation of youth at the present time. There is, as anyone can see, a vast reservoir of moral idealism, a fervent eagerness to participate in liberating causes, and an almost unlimited willingness to engage in sacrifice if the cause justifies it, but, in the eyes of the majority of young people, these features of contemporary living have no connection with the Church of Jesus Christ. There are, of course, youth programs in most congregations, and many of these are generously financed, but there is little doubt that most of them are failing to do what needs to be done. The modern Church involves the very young, as it involves a fair proportion of the mature, but the failure in regard to those between these is almost total. This is what must change!

When the failure is so great, it is reasonable to look for some really serious mistake. We soon realize that such a mistake, if it exists, is probably entailed in our philosophy rather than in our methods. Actually, our methods are reasonably good. We provide excellent quarters; we establish coffee houses; we organize camps; we employ counselors. Necessary as these may be, they are grossly insufficient if we start with the wrong major premise. We begin to see how wrong our basic approach may be when we realize that most of our youth programs are set up to *serve youth*. The young people, of course, sense this at once. They know that others are paying for their refreshments and their entertainment. But the tragedy is that entertainment is precisely what they do not need, because it is what they already have in superabundance.

What young people need is· *to be needed*, and to *know* that they are needed. If they could be convinced that the world is plagued with a sense of meaninglessness, and that they can have an answer to confusion and perplexity, their relationship to the Church might be altered radically. In short, the only way to attract youth is to draw them into a ministry! They are now trying, in great numbers, to minister to physical hunger or to overcome racial discrimination, but few have been helped to see that the deepest problems of men and women are spiritual. They have not been told that the human harvest is being spoiled for lack of workers, and that they can be the workers. They have not been told of the toil in which they must engage in order to prepare their minds so that they can be effective in reaching others, and particularly those of their own age, who are harassed and helpless.

The Christian faith does not need to go outside itself in order to find a principle which can produce a radical change in the attraction of young people. The principle which is effective, when seriously applied, is inherent in the moral revolution which Christ came to inaugurate. There is no way to exaggerate either the theoretical or practical importance of the words, "The Son of Man also came not to be served but to serve" (Mark 10:45). Modern youth will not be enrolled in the Christian Cause until they are recruited as members of the servant team, ministering to the varied needs of God's children. The motivation for this service is greater with the pattern of the Church than within that of any social agency, because Christ speaks to inner as well as outer needs. Preparation for this kind of ministry is necessarily difficult and long, but that only makes it appealing to the best of our young people.

Though great numbers of young people are wholly outside the life of the Church at this moment, this can change rapidly, as it has changed before. In many areas the moral debacle is so great that a shift of the pendulum is almost inevitable. The obvious weakness of a permissive morality, which is ultimately self-destructive, may lead to a new Puritanism. If it is a Puritanism like that of John Milton who "was made for whatever is arduous," that will constitute an advance of genuine magnitude. Already there are signs that this is beginning to occur, and frequently the young people are more advanced on this road than are their teachers. Some who have discovered at first hand the fact that the pseudo-gods, such as drugs and promiscuity, are fundamentally delusive, are turning, with open eyes, to the Living God.

To some Christians it appears that the major choices of Christian belief are limited to Fundamentalism and Liberalism. By Fundamentalism is meant a position which its upholders suppose identical with historic orthodoxy, though often this is not the case. We do not, of course, hear the word Fundamentalism very much today, the word having gone out of fashion, but large numbers still adhere to what the term once denoted. The major mark of this position is strict literalism about the Holy Scriptures. Reacting, understandably, against the superficiality of religion in general, people recognize that they need something firm and it is, they assert, found in an unabashed Biblicism. Adherence is given to any doctrine, if the Bible supposedly teaches it.

The position just mentioned has relatively little support among the most influential religious leaders, but it is still the position of millions of people who have few able spokesmen. Part of the sadness of the religious scene is that there is often no real communication between masses of modest Christians and the ecumenical leaders, who are more truly isolated than they realize.

The major difficulty of Fundamentalism, by whatever name, is its inability to give an intelligible account of the Christian faith. Seldom does it indicate clearly how it is possible to be a sincere Christian and also to accept the major conclusions of natural science. It is not necessary to adopt scientism, or the idolatry of science, to understand that science is here to stay. The combination of science and technology, which made possible the landing of men on the moon, is something which every reverent man is bound to honor. Somehow, if we are to live intelligently, we must find a way to hold, without incompatability, reverence for the Creator and also the major findings of geology and the other sciences. The unfortunate fact is that this is something which the strict Biblicist cannot do.

Though many proclaim their Biblical literalism with confidence, it is soon evident, when we make careful inquiry, that the alleged literalism is actually held with reservations or with ambiguity. In practice, people choose which passages they elect to take literally, and which ones they elect to interpret metaphorically. It seems impossible, for example, to find anyone, in spite of his protestations, who interprets baptism by fire in a nonfigurative fashion. A good example of the problem which the literalist faces is that presented by the words of the Apostle Paul when he is definite on a number of subjects, such as the superiority of the unmarried state (I Cor. 7:7), and the subordination of women. How many are there, in fact, who accept without qualifications the assertion that, if there is anything women desire to know, "let them ask their husbands at home" (I Cor. 14:35)? If the literalist dismisses this unambiguous imperative by saying that it applied only to a particular situation, where there was a special problem of overtalkative women, he has already undermined his own general position.

Much as we may admire the sincere devotion and sacrificial giving of many persons in the Fundamentalist camp, we must conclude that theirs is not a live option in the contemporary world. The Christian does not dare to take a stand which he cannot accept with the concurrence of all of his mental powers. We do not know very much, but we at least know that we must avoid obscurantism. The Christian faith is disloyal to its own genius whenever it undertakes to prevent enlightenment.

In the thinking of many persons, the only alternative to Fundamentalism is some form of Liberalism. Because, by the very nature of the care, Liberalism is a varied phenomenon, it is harder to describe than is Fundamentalism, but the general form is recognizable. Liberalism is marked, for the most part, not by what is believed, but by what is not believed. For example, one who labels himself a liberal Christian may not believe in the inerrancy of the Scriptures, in the virgin birth, in the bodily resurrection of Christ, or in the Second Coming of Christ. The spectrum of Liberalism is so wide, however, that it may include many more negations than those just mentioned, some of which are far more extreme. Thus it is not uncommon to find clergymen who reject the possibility of miracles or of the resurrection of Christ.

The chief way in which all Liberalism is vulnerable is that it is inherently ambiguous. As a mood of openness to new truth from whatever quarter, it is unassailable, and must therefore be part of any honest approach to the truth. If a liberal is one who draws his conclusions upon the basis of evidence and is ready to change when new light appears, then it follows that every person of intellectual integrity is a liberal. But the situation is entirely different if we are talking about a creed. Some assert that the one positive feature of the liberal faith is the dignity of man, but this only raises new questions. Anyone with a philosophical bent is aware that the doctrine of human worth is one which cannot stand alone, all of its validity being derivative.

One apparent item of liberal belief is *freedom*, but the trouble is that this may mean anything. "The world," said Lincoln, "has never had a good definition of the word liberty." Complete freedom is complete nonsense, because it includes the right to deny freedom to other people. When anyone says that he believes in freedom, we have no means of knowing whether he refers to *freedom to* or merely *freedom from*. If he means the latter, there is no positive content in his faith, while, if he means the former, he is valuing something else above freedom, and this is determinative of his conduct.

Ambiguous as the liberal creed may be, it is only fair to

point out that many Christians, who espouse the liberal cause, are obviously sincere and have a valuable contribution to make. Even their negativity is a reaction to something which seems to them evil. Many of these have been touched by the spirit of Christ and they are trying, consequently, to relate to the contemporary needs of perplexed men and women. As we observe the Christian scene, we recognize that persons tend to classify themselves as liberals, not because they actually have a liberal creed, but because they are in honorable revolt against close-mindedness. Liberalism, at its best, is therefore a matter of mood.

It is a striking fact that, for the most part, the greatest decline in Christian vitality is shown today by those groups which pride themselves upon their Liberalism and upon little else. This is not really surprising, since people will dedicate their lives only to something that is positive. People are not held together very long by a consideration of what they do not believe. Note that the erosion of faith, which caught public attention for a brief period when "Christian atheism" was seriously proposed, was the logical result of certain liberal tendencies. Once the first step of denying that God is a Person has been taken, there is not much to keep people from moving further in the same direction until they deny God completely.

Fortunately, an antiquated Fundamentalism and a largely sterile Liberalism do not exhaust the practical possibilities of the Christian Cause. One of the most heartening facts of our particular time is that a genuine third option is coming into being. The third option, which is developing with impressive speed, may best be termed the New Evangelicalism. The Church which is envisaged for the future will, we are told, be *catholic, evangelical,* and *reformed.*

Selections in Chapter Ten are taken from:
The Future of the Christian

Make me thy servant, Lord,
Where e'er my place may be;
Help me to think aright,
My duty now to see.

Use, Lord, my human voice
To reach some one in need;
Employ my human hands,
The hungry now to feed.

Inflame my heart, I pray,
Till I am wholly thine;
Teach me to live and learn,
Until thy will is mine.

—D. Elton Trueblood

Books By D. Elton Trueblood

The Essence Of Spiritual Religion 1936
The Trustworthiness Of Religious Experience 1939
The Knowledge of God 1939
The Logic Of Belief 1942
The Predicament Of Modern Man 1944
Foundations For Reconstruction 1946
Dr. Johnson's Prayers 1947
Alternative To Futility 1948
The Common Ventures Of Life 1949
The Signs Of Hope In A Century Of Despair 1950
The Life We Prize 1951
Your Other Vocation 1952
The Recovery Of Family Life
   (with Pauline Trueblood) 1953
Declaration of Freedom 1955
Philosophy Of Religion 1957
The Yoke Of Christ 1958
The Idea Of A College 1959
Confronting Christ 1960
The Company Of The Committed 1961
General Philosophy 1963
The Humor Of Christ 1964
The Lord's Prayers 1965
The People Called Quakers 1966
The Incendiary Fellowship 1967
Robert Barclay 1968
A Place To Stand 1969
The New Man For Our Time 1970
The Future Of The Christian 1971
The Validity Of The Christian Mission 1972
Abraham Lincoln: Theologian Of American Anguish 1973
While It Is Day: An Autobiography 1974

BIBLIOGRAPHY

The editor and publisher wish to express appreciation to Harper & Row, Publishers, Inc., for permission to excerpt the following copyrighted materials:

From: ALTERNATIVE TO FUTILITY by Elton Trueblood. Copyright, 1948 by Harper & Row, Publishers, Inc. Reprinted by permission of Harper & Row, Publishers, Inc.

From: THE LIFE WE PRIZE by Elton Trueblood. Copyright, 1951 by Harper & Row, Publishers, Inc. Reprinted by permission of Harper & Row, Publishers, Inc.

From: THE PREDICAMENT OF MODERN MAN by Elton Trueblood. Copyright, 1944 by Harper & Row, Publishers, Inc. Reprinted by permission of Harper & Row, Publishers, Inc.

From: THE RECOVERY OF FAMILY LIFE by Elton Trueblood and Pauline Trueblood. Copyright, 1953 by Harper & Row, Publishers, Inc. Reprinted by permission of Harper & Row, Publishers, Inc.

From: YOUR OTHER VOCATION by Elton Trueblood. Copyright, 1952 by Harper & Row, Publishers, Inc. Reprinted by permission of Harper & Row, Publishers, Inc.

From: THE YOKE OF CHRIST by Elton Trueblood. Copyright © 1958 by David Elton Trueblood. Reprinted by permission of Harper & Row, Publishers, Inc.

From: A PLACE TO STAND by Elton Trueblood. Copyright © 1969 by David Elton Trueblood. Reprinted by permission of Harper & Row, Publishers, Inc.

From: CONFRONTING CHRIST by Elton Trueblood. Copyright © 1960 by David Elton Trueblood. Reprinted by permission of Harper & Row, Publishers, Inc.

From: WHILE IT IS DAY: AN AUTOBIOGRAPHY by Elton Trueblood. Copyright © 1974 by Elton Trueblood. Reprinted by permission of Harper & Row, Publishers, Inc.

SOURCES

The page numbers cited below refer to the paperback editions of Elton Trueblood's works currently available in American bookstores.

Chapter One

Alternative to Futility pp. 61–67
The Company of the Committed pp. 1–2, 9–10, 15, 17, 21–22, 22–23, 26, 31, 34, 36, 38–39, 44, 94, 97–98
The Incendiary Fellowship pp. 15, 22, 24, 25, 100, 101, 111
The Life We Prize p. 164
The Yoke of Christ pp. 21, 87

Chapter Two

Confronting Christ p. 11
The Life We Prize pp. 201–202
A Place to Stand pp. 38, 39–40, 41–42, 43–44, 51–53, 111–113, 122–124, 127–128
The Trustworthiness of Religious Experience pp. 9–11
The Validity of the Christian Mission p. 64
The Yoke of Christ pp. 76–79

Chapter Three

The Common Ventures of Life pp. 35–36
The Life We Prize pp. 51–52
The New Man for Our Time pp. 30–31, 32–34, 38–39, 40, 41, 57–58
A Place to Stand pp. 31–34

Chapter Four

Chapter Five

Chapter Six

Chapter Seven

Chapter Eight

Chapter Nine

Chapter Ten